# The Art of Relationship Communication

5 Steps to Enhanced Communication and Relationship Skills

By Margo Hamilton

© **Copyright 2024 - All rights reserved.**

The content contained within this book may not be reproduced, duplicated or transmitted without direct written permission from the author or the publisher.

Under no circumstances will any blame or legal responsibility be held against the publisher, or author, for any damages, reparation, or monetary loss due to the information contained within this book, either directly or indirectly.

Legal Notice:

This book is copyright protected. It is only for personal use. You cannot amend, distribute, sell, use, quote or paraphrase any part, or the content within this book, without the consent of the author or publisher.

Disclaimer Notice:

Please note the information contained within this document is for educational and entertainment purposes only. All effort has been executed to present accurate, up to date, reliable, complete information. No warranties of any kind are declared or implied. Readers acknowledge that the author is not engaged in the rendering of legal, financial, medical or professional advice. The content within this book has been derived from various sources. Please consult a licensed professional before attempting any techniques outlined in this book.

By reading this document, the reader agrees that under no circumstances is the author responsible for any losses, direct or indirect, that are incurred as a result of the use of the information contained within this document, including, but not limited to, errors, omissions, or inaccuracies.

Thank you for purchasing this book.
If you've enjoyed it we'd love if you could
leave a review. The QR code below will take you there.

Your support of Independent Publishers is greatly appreciated.

Well wishes
The Modern Flow Collective

www.modernflowcollective.com

# Table of Contents

**INTRODUCTION** ........................................................................................... 1

**CHAPTER 1: THE IMPORTANCE OF COMMUNICATION IN RELATIONSHIPS** ...................... 7
   *Communication—The Cornerstone of Any Relationship*............................. 7
   *How Childhood Influenced Your Default Communication Style* ................ 9
   *Overview of Common Communication Pitfalls* ........................................ 11
   *Benefits of Mastering Communication Skills* ........................................... 13
   *Journal Prompt* ........................................................................................ 16

**STEP 1: UNDERSTANDING YOURSELF** ................................................................. 17

**CHAPTER 2: SELF-AWARENESS AND EMOTIONAL INTELLIGENCE** ............................. 19
   *Identifying Your Attachment/Communication Style* ................................ 19
   *The Role of Attachment Theory in Communication* ................................ 23
   *Exercises for Increasing Self-Awareness* .................................................. 25
   *Journal Prompt* ........................................................................................ 28

**CHAPTER 3: MANAGING YOUR EMOTIONS** ........................................................ 29
   *Understanding Triggers and Your Emotional Responses* ......................... 29
   *Putting a Name to Emotions* .................................................................... 31
   *Techniques for Emotional Regulation* ...................................................... 33
   *The Impact of Unmanaged Emotions on Communication* ...................... 35
   *Journal Prompt* ........................................................................................ 37

**STEP 2: UNDERSTANDING YOUR PARTNER** ........................................................ 39

**CHAPTER 4: RECOGNIZING YOUR OWN AND YOUR PARTNER'S COMMUNICATION STYLE** ... 41
   *How to Identify Communication/Attachment Styles* .............................. 41
   *Common Misunderstandings Between Different Styles* ......................... 44
   *Adapting Your Communication to Suit Your Partner's Style* .................. 46
   *Journal Prompt* ........................................................................................ 50

**CHAPTER 5: EMPATHY AND ACTIVE LISTENING** .................................................. 51
   *The Importance of Empathy in Relationships* .......................................... 51
   *Techniques for Active Listening* ................................................................ 53
   *How to Validate Your Partner's Feelings and Experiences* ....................... 55
   *Journal Prompt* ........................................................................................ 57

**STEP 3: EFFECTIVE COMMUNICATION TECHNIQUES** ........................................... 59

**CHAPTER 6: THE ART OF CONVERSATION** ......................................................... 61
   *Starting and Maintaining Meaningful Conversations* ............................. 61
   *Balancing Speaking and Listening* ........................................................... 63
   *Navigating Small Talk and Deep Conversations* ..................................... 65
   *Journal Prompt* ........................................................................................ 66

## Chapter 7: Nonverbal Communication .................................................. 69
- The Power of Body Language, Tone, and Facial Expressions .......... 69
- How to Read and Respond to Nonverbal Cues ................................ 72
- Synchronizing Verbal and Nonverbal Messages .............................. 74
- Journal Prompt ................................................................................ 76

## Chapter 8: Conflict Resolution ............................................................. 77
- Understanding the Role of Conflict in Relationships ...................... 77
- Strategies for Healthy Conflict Resolution ..................................... 78
- Turning Conflicts Into Opportunities for Growth ........................... 80
- Journal Prompt ................................................................................ 82

# STEP 4: BUILD STRONGER CONNECTIONS ................................... 85

## Chapter 9: Building Trust and Intimacy ............................................... 87
- The Role of Trust in Communication .............................................. 87
- Practices for Building and Maintaining Trust ................................. 88
- Enhancing Emotional and Physical Intimacy Through Communication ....... 90
- Journal Prompt ................................................................................ 92

## Chapter 10: Setting Boundaries and Respecting Limits ...................... 93
- The Importance of Boundaries in Relationships ............................ 93
- Communicating Boundaries Effectively ......................................... 96
- Respecting Your Partner's Boundaries .......................................... 98
- Journal Prompt .............................................................................. 100

## Chapter 11: Communicating Love and Appreciation ........................ 101
- Expressing Love and Appreciation in Everyday Interactions ....... 101
- Understanding and Speaking Your Partner's Love Language ...... 103
- The Impact of Gratitude on Relationship Satisfaction ................. 105
- Journal Prompt .............................................................................. 106

# STEP 5: PRACTICAL APPLICATIONS ............................................. 107

## Chapter 12: Communication in Different Relationship Stages ........ 109
- Early Relationship Communication .............................................. 109
- Communicating During Major Life Changes ................................ 111
- Long-Term Relationship Communication .................................... 113
- Journal Prompt .............................................................................. 115

## Chapter 13: Exercises and Practice ................................................... 117
- Practical Exercises for Improving Communication Skills ............. 117
- Role–Playing Scenarios for Conflict Resolution ........................... 119
- Journaling Prompts: Positive Self–Talk and Growth .................... 121

# CONCLUSION: THE JOURNEY OF CONTINUOUS IMPROVEMENT ..... 123

# REFERENCES ................................................................................... 125

# Introduction

As much as we'd like them to be, relationships aren't always straightforward. It would be great if the math of relationship was a case of simply giving and receiving love in equal measure. We each enter the relationship with our subjective expectations, emotional baggage, and unique perspective crafted by our previous love ventures and childhood experiences. Even though we're grown-ups, the blueprint for our relationships is often formed by what we witnessed between our caregivers. If we saw healthy, communicative interactions, that's fantastic! It equips us with strong foundations for our own connections. But even if our caregivers' relationship wasn't ideal, we shouldn't despair! Communication is a skill not only worth having, but one that can be constantly chiseled, improved, and applied for relationship success.

I'm Margo, a self-help writer driven by a core belief: communication holds the key to unlocking the true potential of our relationships. It wasn't a textbook or a lecture that sparked my passion for communication in relationships; it was real life. Witnessing firsthand how powerful, honest conversations could completely reshape connections between people left a lasting impact. I saw friends reconnect after years of estrangement, simply because they finally opened up and listened to each other. I watched couples move from frustration to understanding through clear and heartfelt communication. These moments ignited a fire within me—a desire to help others experience the same transformative power.

Being an empathetic person has always been a part of who I am. I find myself naturally drawn to understanding the emotions of those around me. This ability to connect and pick up on what people are feeling is almost involuntary, but empathy without action felt incomplete. Realizing this, it became clear: I had to use this gift to extend a helping hand.

My ongoing research dives into the fascinating world of communication styles and attachment theory. It's here that I explore how these fundamental elements act as building blocks for our relationships and personal growth. It's undeniable and quite exciting to observe how our backgrounds and childhood experiences leave a lasting mark. They shape how we express ourselves, listen to others, and ultimately, connect. But here's the empowering truth: we are not bound by these initial patterns. My research delves into the exciting potential for transformation. If we choose to do the work, we can evolve these communication styles and attachment behaviors. It's a journey of self-discovery, and the good news is that we all have the capacity for growth.

I see our lives and relationships not as fixed destinations, but as ongoing journeys. Every interaction, and every conversation becomes an opportunity for learning and growth. By understanding communication styles and attachment theory, we can navigate these opportunities with greater awareness, ultimately enriching our experiences in profound ways.

Allow me to act as your guide and help you navigate the beautiful, yet complex, landscape of human connection. My focus is on empowering you to embrace authentic communication, as it's the secret ingredient, the cornerstone of building truly thriving relationships. Whether it's navigating difficult conversations or simply fostering deeper understanding, I'll provide you with the tools and strategies that will aid you in connecting with yourself and others on a more meaningful level.

We are all wired for connection—it's a fundamental need, as essential as air or water. But, as acclaimed emotion researcher Brené Brown masterfully points out in *Atlas of the heart*, simply *fitting in* doesn't really cut it (2021). We crave the feeling of *belonging*, of being truly understood and accepted by others without judgment. This doesn't mean having the same personality or sharing all of our hobbies. It's more about complementing each other and not only cherishing our differences, but seeing them as elements that have the potential to make our relationship stronger and sustainable. This is the kind of connection that brings us joy, security, and a sense of purpose.

However inconvenient it may be, the connection doesn't just happen. It requires a bridge, a way to cross the gap between ourselves and others, and that bridge is communication. Without it, we're left isolated, stranded on our own islands of experience. We might see others, and smile politely, but there's no true understanding, no shared journey. Let's think about it this way: Two people facing each other, each lost in their own thoughts, so no words are spoken, no gestures exchanged. There's a physical presence, but no connection. Now, imagine them starting a conversation. They share stories, listen actively, and respond with empathy. A spark ignites, and a bridge is built. Suddenly, they're no longer isolated individuals, but connected beings experiencing the world together.

Without the constant flow of information, emotions, and needs that keeps connections strong and vibrant, misunderstandings can fester, and we leave the door open for negativity to creep in. When feelings and needs go unexpressed, a partner might feel unheard, unimportant, or even rejected. While all this is unintentional, it's not difficult to imagine what it feels like when your partner is constantly working late without explanation. You might feel rejected, assuming they don't care about spending time together. What if you knew the cause of their being less present in the relationship? How different would that feel? Without clear communication, assumptions run wild. Body language is misinterpreted, tones are misconstrued, and intentions are misunderstood. Wouldn't life as a whole be easier if we just communicated better with each other?

Because how we use words shapes how we feel, but words without context are too ambiguous to be meaningful, this book goes beyond the simple act of exchanging words. It delves into the deeper aspects of communication, equipping you to build stronger relationships and foster deeper connections, and we'll start with what's at hand—you. The journey begins with self-awareness, and by the time you're done reading the first part, you'll be able to identify your own communication style, strengths, and weaknesses. This section will guide you in exploring your emotional triggers and how they might influence your communication. Through self-reflection exercises and journaling prompts, you'll gain a deeper understanding of your needs and desires, allowing you to express them clearly and confidently in your interactions.

However, because communication isn't a one-way street, section two emphasizes the importance of active listening and developing empathy for those you connect with. It will equip you with techniques to truly hear what others are saying, both verbally and nonverbally. You'll learn to identify their emotions, understand their perspectives—as different as they might be from yours—and respond with compassion.

The next three parts take a step beyond theory, and empower you to put everything into practice and implement positive change in your own communication style. This is where you'll find the practical tools and strategies that you can integrate into your daily interactions. You'll learn to express yourself assertively, navigate difficult conversations with grace, and set healthy boundaries. As you embrace these changes, you'll unlock the potential for stronger relationships that stand the test of time and its many challenges, your confidence will reach new and healthy heights, and living a more fulfilling life will be entirely in your power.

Whether you seek this out or not, by embodying the principles of effective communication, you become a role model for those around you. We all want to learn and imitate something we perceive as positive and useful, don't we? Once you approach conflicts with an open mind, actively listen to understand rather than respond, and express your emotions constructively, you inspire others to adopt more positive communication habits, fostering a ripple effect of connection and understanding within your relationships.

The most transformative element in your life lies within you, and it's your commitment to positive change. After you read this book, you'll feel empowered to grab the reins of your life and take action. With each conversation you approach with these newfound skills, with each difficult situation you navigate with grace, you unlock the power of healthy communication for both of you. The rewards are profound and are within your reach—stronger relationships, increased confidence, and a life enriched by meaningful connections.

So, are you ready to embark on this journey? Let's metaphorically and literally turn the page and begin building a world where communication fosters understanding, connection, and a sense of belonging for all.

Let's turn our relationships into those healthy and honest connections that propel us to reach our full potential.

Chapter 1:
# The Importance of Communication in Relationships

No matter the rollercoaster of life, every relationship, but especially romantic ones, thrive on open communication. It's the key to sharing burdens, cheering each other on, and tackling challenges as a team. When conversations dry up, tempers run short, worries fester, support fades, and disagreements turn into battles. However, the most simple solution might lie in our ability to open up to the other's perspective and in focusing on *us*, by truly listening, with our ears and heart.

## Communication—The Cornerstone of Any Relationship

What feels like an eternity ago, Dr. John Gottman, a leading expert in relationships, made a groundbreaking discovery: a couple's communication style can be a powerful predictor of their relationship's success (1999). Effective communication goes far beyond the stringing together of words, and we'll dive deep into this slightly later in the book, but it's worth mentioning that tone of voice, body language, facial expressions, and even silence—all forms of nonverbal communication can speak volumes. A raised eyebrow can convey skepticism, a slumped posture might indicate disinterest, just as well as a warm smile can instantly build trust. In many cases, what's left unsaid can be just as impactful, or even more so, than the spoken word.

This is not to say that words aren't important. I should know, right? I juggle them all day long, but while the recipe for a successful relationship might be as different as the number of couples out there, (spicy salsa versus tzatziki), there are some core ingredients that are common across the board (and I don't mean cucumbers):

- Truly listening to each other: Trust hinges on gifting our loved one our full and undivided attention. Only this way can we engage in active listening—truly focusing on their words and needs, summarizing, and compassionately clarifying everything that we're uncertain about. This builds a safe space for honest conversations, swapping judgment for understanding.

- Not taking everything personally: When we become great communicators, we cease seeing our partner's actions as a direct affront to us. We gain the ability to shift our focus to understanding the situation and collaboratively finding solutions that work for both of us.

- The defusing power of "I" statements: Let's ditch the blame game! When frustrated, use "I feel" statements. Replace "You never do the laundry," with "I feel overwhelmed when laundry mounds up. Can we discuss how to share laundry tasks?" This opens the door for a solution-oriented conversation.

- Kindness is always a good idea: We all have those days when everything just seems to go wrong, and we snap at the ones we love. But remember, our partner has bad days too. Instead of getting caught up in blame or frustration, let's practice kindness. Imagine how you'd feel if the roles were reversed. Wouldn't you appreciate understanding and a little patience? Extending kindness doesn't mean ignoring issues, but in the moment, it can defuse tension and open the door for a more compassionate conversation later.

- Put acceptance on the menu: Healthy communication isn't about forcing agreement. It's about acknowledging and validating our partner's feelings, even if we see things differently. Respecting their right to their emotions, however different from ours, creates a safe space for open dialogue and a stronger connection.

Strong communication in relationships goes beyond playing ping-pong with words. It's about creating a space where both partners can freely express their needs and feel genuinely heard. When you can effectively communicate what you need and respond with empathy to your partner's needs, a sense of understanding, validation, and deep connection blossoms. You can both let your guard down now because you trust each other not to exploit the areas where you still feel challenged and help each other build yourselves up.

Remember, communication isn't about bottling up emotions or winning arguments. It's about aiming to understand each other's perspectives and honoring them. There's so much we can learn from each other, if only we listened to each other with a non–judgmental ear. However, if communication feels like a hurdle at first, please know that it isn't something you should blame yourself or your partner for, but on the contrary, focus your efforts in believing and acting on the principle that communication is something that can be improved upon and practiced until it becomes second nature and healthy for everybody involved.

## How Childhood Influenced Your Default Communication Style

Thinking back to our childhoods, we were likely taught valuable lessons about respect: don't interrupt, listen to elders, and follow instructions. These rules served a purpose, creating a safe environment for learning and growth, but as we mature, communication needs to evolve, and rules have to be adapted to our adult needs. We can't simply apply the same old guides and live in a world where open communication is stifled, where voicing our opinions feels disrespectful, and where asserting our needs is seen as selfish.

Our mind is capable of more complex thoughts, and we can now discern the difference between following instructions blindly, simply because we trust that someone else knows what's better for us, and applying self-awareness and reason to decide ourselves what's best for us. When we still hang onto the same old rules without occasionally updating them with the latest "software", the lack of assertiveness that we feel can lead to resentment, missed opportunities, and difficulty advocating for ourselves in personal and professional settings.

However, even though we can probably all agree those rules are too limited to suit us now, the lessons learned while our personalities were still developing linger with us for a long time, if left unchallenged. All the observations we made before our minds reached our current capacity, feel ingrained in who we are and impact our communication styles.

Childhood is a crucial time for developing communication skills and growing up amid an ocean of mixed messages can be incredibly confusing and impacting. Words don't match actions, so you can't apply logic and reason to figure things out. These situations simply don't make sense. A parent says they love their child, but their actions convey neglect. A friend claims they value you, yet excludes you from social events. This constant dissonance, this confusing inconsistency, creates an environment of distrust and uncertainty, making it difficult to decipher genuine emotions. When bombarded with mixed messages in childhood, it's natural to adopt those same confusing communication patterns. You may find yourself saying *yes* when you mean *no*, or offering lukewarm enthusiasm when you're truly excited. This can leave others feeling bewildered and unable to trust your words.

When you're a child and the key people in your life avoid directness, kindness, and confidence in their communication, such as a caregiver expressing disapproval through passive-aggressive silence, or a friend who uses manipulation to get what they want, things get even more confusing. These indirect communication styles can leave you feeling unheard and confused, struggling to navigate your own voice. Whether you like it or not, this communication style taught you some bad lessons. As an adult, you might become timid, fearing to speak up and missing out, or alternatively, you could become overbearing, compensating for a lack of attention by dominating conversations. Equally damaging, manipulation can also be a consequence, a strategy learned to get what you want but ultimately hurting trust in your relationships.

Another childhood scenario is that in which your opinions might have been dismissed, your questions met with discouragement, and your voice was rarely heard. This lack of inclusion in decision-making or open dialogue creates an environment where healthy communication, understandably, struggles to develop. Effective communication thrives on an equal exchange of ideas and information; It's a two-way street where both speaking and listening are valued. When children are discouraged from expressing their thoughts or asking questions, they miss out on crucial communication skills and valuable practice.

Children who weren't encouraged to speak up may become adults reluctant to share opinions, fearing judgment. The lack of validation they endured can also lead to a lack of confidence in their own ideas, and they might become passive communicators, struggling to initiate conversations or ask questions.

Many are tempted to call these communication styles *dysfunctional*, but I prefer looking on the bright side where there's something we can do about it, and call them *out of alignment*. This means that the communication styles learned during childhood, that have the potential to hinder us from forming deeper connection with others, can be fixed. If we become self-aware of the rules that no longer guide, but hinder, the adult we've grown into has the power to change them.

## Overview of Common Communication Pitfalls

Every single romantic relationship experiences conflict at some point; it's only natural! While constant conflict isn't ideal, healthy disagreements are actually a sign of a strong relationship. Open communication, even when it involves differing viewpoints, allows you to have authentic and honest discussions that lead to deeper understanding and connection. These conversations don't have to be confrontational, but rather a chance to explore each other's perspectives and find solutions that work for both of you.

I used to be a champion rug-sweeper! Brushing aside problems seemed easier at the time, but issues always have a way of bubbling up later, often in a bigger, messier way. Now I know that open communication, even about tough topics, is key. Instead of bottling things up and venting to others, focus on addressing concerns directly with your partner. This allows you to work through things together and prevents passive-aggressive behavior. To my knowledge, mind-reading is still a skill more suited to science fiction than to reality, so why expect it out of our partner?

Other than this volcano of avoidance, here are a few other red flags when it comes to unhealthy communication in relationships:

- Making assumptions in regards to the partner's feelings or thoughts without checking in with them

- Passing the ball of criticism between the two of you

- Passive-aggressive behavior or opinions dressed up as irony, sarcasm, or condescension

- One of you needs to yell to be heard

- Putting up defensive walls when the other tries to talk about something uncomfortable

- The ugliest of them all—prescribing each other the silent treatment

- Verbally fighting about the same issues over and over again

- Compromise is never on the table

The same Dr. Gottman mentioned previously, together with his wife, Julie Gottman, devised over the last five decades an even more straightforward (and catchy) way to recognize the most common relationship communication pitfalls. They called them the Four Horsemen (Gottman & Gottman, 2015):

- **The Critic:** This horseman isn't offering constructive feedback, but rather launching personal attacks on your character, habits, or decisions. This partner constantly saying, "You never (insert hurtful criticism)!" This negativity breeds resentment and drives a wedge between partners.

- **The Defender:** Instead of addressing the issue at hand, the Defender goes on the offensive. They might deny responsibility, make excuses, or even blame their partner. Statements like "It's not my fault that (insert what they've felt accused of), you never help!" are classic examples of defensiveness, shutting down productive conversation.

- **The Horseman of Contempt:** This is the most toxic of the bunch. Contempt involves treating your partner with disrespect, mockery, or even disgust. Sarcastic remarks, name-calling, or eye rolls all convey contempt, eroding trust and affection. Actually, this seems to be the most reliable predictor for divorce (Gottman & Gottman, 2015).

- **The Stonewalling Rider:** This horseman simply shuts down emotionally. They withdraw from conversation, refusing to communicate or address the problem. The silent treatment might seem like a temporary solution, but it leaves issues unresolved and creates a sense of emotional disconnect.

Some of these signs might be more subtle, but others are blasting sirens telling us that the road we're on isn't leading anywhere healthy. Once we recognize these red flags and consciously avoid them, we can cultivate healthier communication patterns. The Four Horsemen aren't harbingers of inevitable doom, they're alarm systems going off and asking us to take immediate, effective, and collaborative action.

## Benefits of Mastering Communication Skills

While it's true that every relationship is unique, and my vision of success can look different to yours, there are undeniable benefits to effective communication that transcend our specific goals.

One of the hidden gems of a successful relationship is less rumination. When you can openly communicate with your partner, you don't have to bottle up negative emotions, which are absolutely normal in any relationship, or dwell on them alone. Talking things through allows you to address concerns constructively, preventing them from spiraling into negativity and overthinking. Talking about such negative occurrences doesn't have to be confrontational; with communication skills, it can simply be a conversation—no feelings getting hurt.

Maybe not surprisingly, researchers found that simply feeling valued by their partner led people to report better sleep (Selcuk et al.,2017). This highlights a powerful truth: good relationships have a profound impact that extends far beyond just emotional well-being. Good relationships aren't just a feel-good bonus; they're a cornerstone of well-being overall. Feeling valued allows us to develop a sense of security, support, and belonging. It fosters a positive outlook and reduces stress, all of which contribute to better sleep and overall physical health.

Another hallmark of a successful relationship is the blossoming of intimacy. This deep emotional connection thrives on good communication, a two-way street of sharing and listening. Effective communication allows for reciprocal self-disclosure, where you both feel comfortable expressing your experiences, beliefs, values, and even vulnerabilities with each other, without the fear of being judged for them. Over time, as communication deepens, so does your understanding and connection, fostering a truly intimate bond.

Regardless of how great communicators we are, we all have triggers, and sometimes our initial reactions aren't our best. It's inevitable that we sometimes slip up, and normally, that would lead to conflict. This isn't the case, however, when we also have the key to resolving them effectively—the same old communication. Let's say you ask your partner to help with a chore, and they sigh dramatically. That sigh might trigger uncomfortable feelings, and our natural tendency is to react and snap back or shut down. However, this often leads to a cycle of negativity.

Effective communication asks us to take a step back. Instead of reacting to triggers, we assess our thoughts and feelings. What's really bothering us about the sigh? Is it the dismissiveness, or a deeper feeling of not being valued? Often, conflict stems from misunderstandings or unmet needs. We get caught up in our partner's actions or responses, but what's driving their behavior? Maybe they're tired, or stressed about something else. This is where we shouldn't fall into the trap of assuming we know what's going on in their brain and simply ask them. By focusing on understanding, we can disarm those initial triggers that clawed themselves to the surface. When we see the world from our partner's perspective, the sigh might not feel like a personal attack, but a sign of something else entirely. This deeper connection reduces the power of triggers and fosters a more peaceful conflict resolution.

Healthy communication requires curiosity, both about ourselves and our partner. What are we feeling? Why is our partner reacting this way? Asking open-ended questions and actively listening to their perspective can be a game-changer and the key to effective communication and overall well-being for both of you.

Last but not least, and maybe the most meaningful benefit that can be drawn from effective communication in our long-term relationships, is supporting each other and making both of us more resilient. No relationship is sunshine and rainbows all the time and even if we're lucky and it is, life throws its fair share of curveballs, and sometimes they hit hard. When tough times hit ground, simply being there for your partner can make a world of difference. Imagine facing a difficult situation alone. Now imagine having a hand to hold, a shoulder to cry on, or a listening ear that truly hears you. Effective communication allows you to express your vulnerabilities and anxieties, knowing your partner is there to catch you.

This support that I'm referring to goes beyond just being present or being just a witness. It's about truly and actively listening to our partner's struggles, giving them our undivided attention, validating their feelings, and asking clarifying questions. This creates a safe space for them to express themselves openly and feel understood. Support isn't always verbal. Sometimes, a warm embrace, a helping hand with chores, or simply offering to take on extra responsibilities speaks volumes. Understanding our partner's needs and offering support in ways that resonate with them is key. At the end of the day, challenges, when faced together, can actually strengthen bonds.

However, before we can become those effective communicators that multiply the success potential of our relationships, we need to take a plunge down the rabbit hole and understand ourselves. We can only help others once we've helped ourselves, so, let's find out what are our default communication and attachment styles, how they might pose a challenge in relationships, and all in all, become more self-aware of our needs and values.

## Journal Prompt

As promised, each chapter will have a section where I encourage you to take some time for self-reflection. It might not seem like much the first time you do it, but there's something so pragmatic about translating the ideas that we juggle in our minds and putting them into words on paper (or any digital alternative you prefer). This is the single most effective way to become and stay aware of our inner world.

However, one word of caution, that inner critic will occasionally appear, but we won't have a seat for it at the table. Once you start journaling, refrain from passing judgment on your thoughts. Simply write them as they come even if they come adorned with typos. This is for your eyes only. appear

Now, for the first journaling prompts: Think of a time where you didn't communicate well within your relationship. What was the knock on effect of this? Now, think about a time you communicated effectively in a relationship. What made it successful?

# Step 1: Understanding Yourself

# Chapter 2:
# Self-Awareness and Emotional Intelligence

Many people still dismiss emotional intelligence as something far inferior to the better-known intelligence quotient (IQ), but when it comes to relationships—and in our society, there are plenty of those we all need to navigate—it is emotional intelligence that makes this social world go around. So, when I mention emotional intelligence, and I see people shrug it off as something insignificant, I remember Aristotle's wise words: ""Anyone can become angry—that is easy. But to be angry with the right person, to the right degree, at the right time, for the right purpose, and in the right way—that is not easy" (2012).

Strong relationships thrive on emotional intelligence in general, but if we were to be more precise, it is self-awareness that this foundation is built upon. Knowing yourself (self-awareness) helps you manage your emotions and respond thoughtfully, not impulsively, even when the situation rubs you the wrong way. This emotional control lets you truly hear your partner, empathize and understand their perspective (emotional intelligence), and build trust or find a resolution through open communication.

## Identifying Your Attachment/Communication Style

Attachment theory delves right into the core of human connection, exploring the long–term emotional bonds we form with others, particularly those established in childhood. It goes beyond simply describing these bonds—it explains how our earliest relationships with caregivers shape our emotional patterns and communication styles throughout our entire life.

However, just like all concepts and sciences that deal with people and their behavior, the concept of attachment evolved over time. In the early days, thinkers like Freud believed it was all about satisfying basic needs. They proposed that babies, particularly those in the oral stage focused on feeding and formed attachments with caregivers who provided those necessities. Similarly, some early behavioral theories saw attachment as a learned response to feeding. The idea was that babies were attached to caregivers simply because they were the ones who provided nourishment, so they were the ones helping them survive.

The field of attachment theory wouldn't be what it is today without John Bowlby, a pioneering British psychologist. His observations challenged earlier theories and saw attachment as a deep and lasting emotional bond between people, more than just a fulfillment of needs. He noticed that children separated from their caregivers exhibited significant anxiety, regardless of whether their physical needs were met. This led him to believe attachment wasn't simply about feeding; it was about seeking comfort and security from a trusted caregiver as something instilled in them throughout evolution (Bowlby, 1982).

There are so many things that can be said about attachment theory, and believe me, it takes all my self–control not to go even deeper into the subject, but if you are as interested in it as I am, know that I plan a future book that will be fully dedicated to the subject. So, long story short, to understand attachment theory, imagine a time when staying close to a caregiver meant the difference between life and death for a child. Over generations, through natural selection, humans developed a powerful drive to form attachments and it is this that motivates children to stay close to their caregivers for comfort and protection.

Attachment theory's core idea is this: responsive and available caregivers create a safe haven for their babies. This sense of security allows the child to learn that their caregiver is reliable. Just like a secure base camp for an explorer, this secure attachment gives the child the confidence to venture out and explore the world, knowing they can always return for comfort and support.

Attachment theory identifies four main patterns that form in early childhood:

- **Ambivalent (or anxious) attachment:** Children with this style experience significant distress when a caregiver leaves. This is because, due to inconsistent or unpredictable caregiving, they haven't learned to fully trust their caregiver's availability. They might seem angry or clingy, unsure if their needs will be met.

While not the most common, ambivalent attachment affects an estimated 7-15% of children in the US (Lyons–Ruth, 1996).

- **Avoidant attachment:** These children are withdrawn and avoid seeking comfort from their caregivers. They might even show little difference in their reactions to a familiar caregiver and a stranger. This behavior can develop in response to caregivers who are emotionally distant, neglectful, or even abusive. If a child's attempts to connect are consistently rejected or punished, they might learn to avoid seeking help or closeness altogether.

- **Disorganized attachment:** These children exhibit confusing and contradictory behaviors. They might seem disoriented, dazed, or confused when interacting with their caregiver. One moment, they might seek comfort, but the next, they might avoid or resist any interaction. This inconsistency often stems from caregivers who display mixed signals themselves. Imagine a parent who is sometimes a source of comfort and sometimes a source of fear. This unpredictable behavior leaves the child feeling confused and unsure of how to respond, leading to disorganized attachment.

- **Secure attachment:** The most common attachment style is secure attachment (Moghadam et al., 2016). These children feel confident that their caregivers are dependable. While they might be upset when separated, they trust their caregiver will return. This creates a sense of security that allows them to explore the world freely, knowing they can always come back for comfort and support. When scared, they readily seek reassurance from their caregiver, trusting they'll be soothed and cared for.

While our early attachment styles might evolve over time, they can leave a lasting impression. If you have an anxious attachment style, rooted perhaps in an ambivalent childhood bond, you might find yourself cautious about intimacy. The fear of rejection or a constant need for reassurance can be a hallmark of this style. When it comes to breakups, they're tough for everyone, but for those with anxious attachment, they can be particularly challenging. The worry that your partner's love isn't real or the uncertainty about their feelings can be magnified.

People with avoidant attachment styles often struggle with intimacy and closeness in relationships. Sharing thoughts and feelings can feel uncomfortable, and commitment might seem daunting. This can sometimes manifest as a fear of commitment, and those with this style might appear less emotionally invested in relationships. While this can be a way to shield yourself from getting hurt, it can also hinder the ability to form deep and meaningful connections. Imagine wanting a warm fire on a cold night, but being too afraid to get close to the flames. Avoidant attachment keeps you safe from getting burned, but also prevents you from experiencing the warmth of true intimacy.

Disorganized attachment is characterized by inconsistent and unpredictable behavior in relationships. Someone with this style might be clingy and desperate for closeness one moment, then emotionally distant and withdrawn the next. This confusing pattern often stems from childhood experiences with caregivers whose behavior was erratic or abusive. This inconsistency can make it difficult to build secure and trusting relationships in adulthood.

The good news is that many people develop a secure attachment style and this translates into the ability to build healthy, long-lasting relationships. People with secure attachment typically have good self-esteem, feel comfortable being close to others, they know how to seek support when needed, and are open about their feelings.

Our default attachment style isn't set in stone, and past experiences, even those in challenging relationships, don't have to dictate our future. The beauty of human connection is that we can learn and grow. Old patterns can be unlearned, and new, healthier behaviors can be developed. With openness and a willingness to learn, we can build fulfilling and secure bonds with others.

# The Role of Attachment Theory in Communication

Attachment style, if we were to compare it to a house, is the foundation we built in childhood. While we can remodel and renovate the house to our heart's desire, the foundation stays the same—our attachment style still dictates most of our relationships. However, even though it's time and energy-consuming, foundations can be laid again just as we can work on changing our attachment style if it is one that doesn't encourage deep and meaningful relationships.

## Secure Attachment

The upside of a secure attachment, which is the one we should all strive for, is that of feeling confident and worthy of love, so it's no surprise that people with this style see the best in themselves and others, which helps foster the healthiest of relationships. They're comfortable being both independent and close, striking a perfect balance. Communication is also a breeze because they express themselves clearly and navigate conflict with confidence, knowing it can be resolved through open dialogue. Feedback is always welcomed and never seen as a personal affront, and compromise comes naturally. When a secure attachment is at the core of a relationship, the emotional stability and innate positive outlook on life and connection make it healthy and sustainable.

## Anxious/ Ambivalent Attachment

Anxious attachment is a double–edged sword where we crave both closeness with all our might, but also fear being left behind. We're overly sensitive to any perceived distance or rejection, feelings of abandonment easily creep up on us, and we spend a great amount of time ruminating on perceived rejections. This constant worry fuels our need for reassurance, often leading to anxious communication. This can manifest as nagging, clingy, or smothering behavior, which are really a desperate attempt to feel secure, but one that is understandably unhealthy for everyone involved. While reassurance might soothe anxiety temporarily, it can strain the relationship in the long run.

## Avoidant Attachment

Wanting independence is great, but for those with an avoidant attachment style, it can create an almost unbreachable wall. They struggle to express emotions of all kinds, while fearing intimacy and vulnerability might lead to them being abandoned. The way they see it, vulnerability is a weakness, so they rarely show it. This can leave partners feeling emotionally distant and lead to conflicts. Because of this, relationships become a struggle between needing connection and fearing closeness, thus creating a cycle of loneliness and missed opportunities for deeper bonds.

## Disorganized Attachment

This attachment style is a confusing dance. People with this style crave connection but fear rejection intensely, so they enter into the vicious cycle of wanting closeness and pulling away, but even when they manage to stay in a relationship, they have difficulties communicating their needs and wants. What's characteristic of this attachment style is that they might chase a relationship but then sabotage it or break things off as soon as intimacy deepens. Research even suggests they might have more short-term partners (Favez & Tissot, 2019). Their core challenge is regulating emotions. Learning to manage their thoughts and feelings is the first step towards building healthier, more secure bonds.

The attachment style you developed in your childhood doesn't have to be a lifelong companion. Dedication and having the right tools in hand allow you to transform your relationships and communication patterns. To accomplish this, you first need to do some introspection and find out which attachment style you've developed and what your goals are. Do you crave more intimacy without always fearing rejection? Do you wish to communicate your feelings and needs more effectively? Do you wish to become comfortable while keeping close to people? This is where self–awareness makes your best ally.

# Exercises for Increasing Self-Awareness

At the beginning of this chapter, I mentioned that one of the most important ingredients of a healthy relationship is self-awareness. While it sometimes gets a bad reputation, that happens because it's often misunderstood as being self-centered. However, the way most psychologists understand self-awareness is as an ability to see ourselves clearly, like holding up a mirror to our personality, values, beliefs, and emotions, but not while disregarding everyone else. It's about understanding how our experiences influence our thoughts, actions, and interactions with the world around us.

Just like communication and attachment style, self-awareness is a skill that can be practiced and improved upon. It isn't very different from learning a new language or mastering a musical instrument. Similarly to how learning a language opens doors to new cultures, self-awareness benefits every aspect of our lives by improving our communication skills, strengthening our relationships, and empowering us to make better decisions.

At first, it might feel awkward thinking about ourselves this much, and for many of us, it might be unfamiliar altogether, but with consistency, trial and error, and most importantly, dedication, self-awareness becomes a natural part of who we are—a valuable tool in any social situation.

## Meditation

I'd like to preface this by emphasizing that meditation doesn't necessarily have to be a spiritual practice, but a mental exercise. It's a powerful tool for cultivating self-awareness because it encourages a state of quiet and non–judgmental observation. Unlike other practices that might involve actively changing your thoughts or behaviors, meditation is about simply noticing what's happening within you, acknowledging thoughts and emotions, and letting them "sail away." Think of it as taking a mindful pause to tune into the inner workings of your mind and body.

Two meditation practices that come highly recommended by neurologists, and worked wonders for me and so many people, are mindfulness meditation and body scan (Huberman, 2022). You might have heard of mindfulness meditation as the practice where you focus on being present in the *now*, but to me, it's more like learning to be in tune with your mind and body. Unlike traditional meditation aiming to clear your mind, mindfulness encourages gently observing your thoughts and feelings without judgment. Instead of looking at a recipe composed of thoughts, emotions, behaviors and how they interact, while engaging in mindfulness meditation, you look at a constantly changing ingredient list (consisting these thoughts, emotions, and behaviors), without taking any further action. You notice fleeting thoughts, emotions, and physical sensations without getting caught up in them.

**Mindfulness Exercise**

Decide on a quiet, comfortable place to sit in (somewhere in nature or indoors) and set a timer for five to ten minutes. Start by focusing your attention on your breath and feel the rise and fall of your chest and belly. Then, close your eyes and imagine yourself sitting beside a calm river. Visualize leaves floating gently along the water's surface. As thoughts arise in your mind, picture them landing on leaves. Don't judge the thoughts, simply acknowledge them and watch as the leaves carry them down the river. If a thought grabs your attention, don't be hard on yourself. Just let it go and focus back on the leaves drifting by. This mindfulness exercise helps you detach from your thoughts and cultivate, if not exactly inner peace, then at least equanimity (emotional balance), which is good enough for me.

**Body Scan Exercise**

Find a comfortable position, either lying down or seated, but if this is the first time you're trying this exercise, it's much easier to do it lying down. Close your eyes and take a few slow, deep breaths, feeling your belly rise and fall. Now, shift your attention to your toes and feet. Notice any sensations you might be experiencing, such as tingling, warmth, or pressure against the floor. Breathe deeply and allow your awareness to travel slowly toward the rest of your body. Scan your legs, calves, and thighs, observing any sensations without judgment. Continue moving your awareness throughout your body, exploring your torso, arms, hands, neck, and head. Finally, focus on your body as a whole. Rest in this present moment, awareness for a few breaths before gently starting to move your body and bringing yourself back to the room.

**Investing in Emotional Intelligence**

If self-awareness is the foundation of a strong building, emotional intelligence (EQ) is what you build upon that foundation. Self-awareness is our ability to understand our own emotions, while EQ is our ability to understand and navigate these same emotions when it comes to ourselves and others. Someone with high EQ is like a skilled translator, able to interpret emotional and social cues and respond with the empathy and compassion warranted by the situation and person they're interacting with.

A well developed EQ also allows us to effectively express our own feelings in a healthy way without falling into the trap of remaining silent to avoid outbursts or bottling things up. Essentially, EQ makes us great communicators because it is this emotional agility that allows us to respond thoughtfully and effectively in situations that might otherwise trigger us.

**EQ Boosting Exercise**

Challenge yourself to be a feelings detective throughout your day. When you experience an emotion, pause and ask yourself: "What am I feeling right now?" Identify the specific emotion (frustrated, happy, anxious) and any physical sensations associated with it. Then, consider what might have triggered that feeling. Was it something someone said, a situation you're facing or are about to face, or an internal thought? By regularly practicing this emotional self-awareness, you'll become more adept at identifying, understanding, and managing your own emotions, a key component of emotional intelligence.

Just like meditation and EQ-enhancing exercises, journaling and talk therapy are powerful tools for self-discovery. Through journaling, we can explore our thoughts, feelings, and experiences, gaining insights into our patterns (such as attachment style) and areas for growth. Talk therapy is somewhat similar, but this time, you're becoming a feelings detective under the careful guidance of a professional, and are encouraged to uncover the roots of negative thoughts and behaviors. By understanding the underlying causes of our emotions, behaviors, and default attachment styles, we can develop healthier coping mechanisms and strengthen our self-awareness.

## Journal Prompt

How self–aware are you?

- Can you physically locate where your emotions are present in your body when they arise?

- How do you currently manage your emotions and your reactions to them when they arise?

- Do you reflect on your reactions with the compassion you would show a friend or are you treating yourself as a harsh critic would?

Chapter 3:
# Managing Your Emotions

Emotions are not too dissimilar to rain. They can be as gentle and constant as rain in the fall, they can feel ethereal and put us at ease like snow, or they can be as surprising and intense as a summer downpour. Other times, they might even fly under our radar such as a coastal shower where we're not quite sure if it's drizzling or simply foggy. Our emotions aren't always something that we easily become aware of and label. However, one thing is for sure—they're part of the experience of being us.

## Understanding Triggers and Your Emotional Responses

What makes you smile might leave someone else flat. Not even happiness is a one-size-fits-all emotion—it's a unique blend shaped by our experiences.

How we see the world—our perception and personal interpretation of it—influences our emotional landscape. The same situation can be interpreted as a challenge or an exciting opportunity, depending on our perspective. Resilience, our ability to bounce back after challenges, is another ingredient that highly influences the manifestation of our emotions, just as our preferred coping mechanisms do.

While science tells us emotions involve specific brain regions we all share, such as the amygdala, the way we experience them is deeply personal. It's all about how our own brain interprets the world around us, filtered through our unique lens of perception, resilience, and coping skills. Emotions aren't simply fleeting feelings that don't deserve much of our attention, nor do they only happen in our brains. They're complex and substantially personal experiences that unfold in the entirety of our bodies, our minds, and also in our actions. Psychologists have identified three key components that work together to create the complex experience of human emotion (Kreibig & Gross, 2017):

- **Subjective:** We all share basic (also called universal) emotions like anger or joy, but how we experience them is unique.

Consider anger—it can range from a simmering irritation to explosive rage and these broad labels don't even capture the full range and picture. We often feel blends of emotions, like excitement tinged with nervousness about a new job, or a mix of joy and anxiety around a big life event. These emotions can wash over us simultaneously or one after another, creating a rich and very personal emotional experience.

- **Physiological:** Our emotions have a physical side too. Feelings like anxiety or fear can trigger a cascade of body responses, such as sweaty palms or a racing heart, and all of this is thanks to the autonomic nervous system, which is in charge of our heart rate and digestion. One of its specific branches, the sympathetic nervous system, prepares us for those extreme fight-or-flight situations. While early research focused on these bodily reactions, newer studies focused on exploring the brain's role. Brain scans show that the amygdala lights up both when we see scary things in a movie and when we feel we're in danger (Šimić et al., 2021).

- **Behavioral:** Our emotions might be traversing our minds and bodies, but they come alive through our actions. This is the behavioral response—how we convey our emotions through facial expressions, body language, and even tone of voice. We're constantly deciphering these signals in others and seek to adjust our attitude accordingly, which ties into emotional intelligence, but interestingly, culture plays a role too. Western cultures might openly express excitement or anger, while Eastern cultures might value more subtle expressions. So, the way we show our emotions is a fascinating mix of biology and cultural learning.

Emotions are our body's built-in (internal and external) communication system. When we're feeling afraid, our body interprets sensory inputs (such as someone frowning in our general direction) as a threat, triggering action. But emotions are more than just a feeling; they are a way to spark a chain reaction that fuels learning and growth. Research shows emotions are crucial for cognitive processes like memory, reasoning, and problem-solving—all essential for navigating life and becoming a well-rounded person (Tying et al., 2017).

However, we can all attest that emotions aren't as neat as we'd like them to be. We're content one moment, and then something happens—somebody does something that rubs us the wrong way, or we remember we need to do something that should have been finished yesterday—and contentment morphs into anxiety, mild anger, or frustration. These emotional triggers are invisible tripwires in our minds and can be anything from a specific word to a certain smell, a place, or even a situation that throws us right back into a past experience and sparks an intense emotional reaction.

While we'll delve into how to recognize emotion and triggers in a moment, the key thing to remember is that these triggers aren't about the present moment. They're about unresolved emotions from the past that get hijacked by something in our current situation. For instance, someone who was harshly criticized as a child might feel a surge of anger or shame when receiving feedback at work, even if the feedback is constructive. This is why personal experience is the lens through which we experience the world, at least until we start challenging the beliefs that we mindlessly appropriated from those experiences.

## Putting a Name to Emotions

Naming our emotions doesn't get the stellar reputation it deserves. Naming them simply weakens their grip, like calming a storm, and psychologist Dan Siegel supports this by encouraging us: "name it to tame it" (Siegel, 2014). Brené Brown, who I mentioned before, also favors this mentality by saying "When we name an emotion or experience, it doesn't give that emotion or experience more power, it gives *us* more power" (Brown, 2021).

Ignoring emotions doesn't make them vanish, as much as we'd like to turn a blind eye to them. They're more stubborn than us, and they just linger and impact us. Instead, acknowledging them lets us step back and choose healthy ways to manage them. Think of emotions as energy that needs an outlet. Sharing them, even the tough ones, helps us control them better. By simply saying what's going on inside, we take ownership and prevent them from exploding later.

A UCLA experiment tested the power of naming emotions that are available to all of us. Dr. Craske and her team exposed people scared of spiders to a tarantula and then divided them into groups. The first group simply described their feelings (e.g., "scared of this spider"), while the others were instructed to downplay their fear ("it can't hurt me"), say irrelevant things, or stay silent. A week later, everyone faced the spider again. The group who labeled their fear got significantly closer, showed less distress, and even sweated less, which is a clear sign of reduced fear (Kircanski et al., 2012). This suggests that simply acknowledging our emotions can be surprisingly powerful in managing them.

Because having emotions has been built into us through our evolution as human beings, it is in acknowledging and naming them correctly that can make all the difference. Two emotions that seem to be entwined and are omnipresent, are fear and stress. While being instantly reactive to the two has ensured our survival—there's no conversation to be had with a hungry lion eyeing you—but this fight or flight response, the intensity of stress we experience to situations that get out of control, is often misinterpreted as something more extreme than the situation warrants. This is where we can break the vicious cycle of emotional trigger and reactivity by engaging in self–awareness and deciding on which shade of stress, or any other emotion, we're actually experiencing. We need to expand our emotional vocabulary and put more appropriate labels on what we're feeling:

- **Stressed:** worried, fearful, dreading, anxious, concerned, terrified, cautious, suspicious, self–conscious, timid, guarded, etc.

- **Angry:** resentful, vengeful, impatient, outraged, hostile, judgmental, repulsed, furious, bitter, exasperated, shocked, disempowered, etc.

- **Joyful:** appreciative, compassionate, calm, glad, loving, contemplative, empowered, confident, energetic, inspired, etc.

See how these emotions are cousins, but not siblings? If you were to only use your logic, would you react the same way to something that makes you feel concerned as you would to being terrified? Becoming aware of our emotions and correctly putting a name to them allows us to "embody" the right behavior for the right situation. We react accordingly and with the intensity warranted by the situation at hand, and not as a chain reaction of something similar that happened during our childhood.

For a free and more extensive list of emotions that will help you identify your own, visit www.modernflowcollective.com/freetools.

## Techniques for Emotional Regulation

If self-awareness is the first step and emotional literacy is the second, emotional regulation is the next in taking the reins of our feelings and reactions. It isn't about stuffing down our feelings, but about honing the art of managing their intensity. By using various techniques, we can influence the emotions we experience and how we express them. Think of it as turning down the emotional volume on a stressful situation or choosing a calming response instead of a knee-jerk reaction. Ultimately, it's about taking charge of our emotional state for a healthier and more mindful way of life.

Emotional volatility can wreak havoc on our lives. When we struggle to manage anger, hurtful words can fly like stray bullets, damaging relationships and requiring repairs. We don't get out unscathed from such a situation either. Emotional regulation isn't just about others; it's about protecting ourselves as well from the pain of unmanaged emotions. Uncontrolled sadness can drag down our well-being, while constant fear can hold us back from new experiences.

Here are a number of tools that are always available to you when the intensity of your emotions gets too uncomfortable for your liking or for when they begin to seem out of your control.

## Take a Step Back and Pause

Our emotions can take us by surprise, leaving us feeling flooded and overwhelmed. The key to managing them might seem counterintuitively simple: create space. Instead of reacting instantly, give yourself a gift—a pause. Take a deep breath and slow down the entire experience. This space between the trigger and your response allows you to acknowledge what just happened and identify the emotion bubbling up. With this awareness, you have the power to choose a more thoughtful response.

## Put on Your Emotions Detective Hat

Whenever you're feeling lost in a whirlwind of emotions, the first step is recognizing them. Many therapists suggest we get more curious about our body's reactions. Is our stomach in knots? Heart pounding? Physical sensations such as these are often tied to emotions, and simply noticing them can create a welcome distraction, lessening the intensity of the feeling. Moreover, we should grab hold of these feelings and trace them as far back as we can. Think of other situations that triggered similar emotions. By understanding the roots of our emotional responses, we gain valuable insight (into our attachment style as well) and can start to manage them more effectively.

## Put Your Vocabulary to Good Use

Once we've identified the physical signs of an emotion, let's take the next step: naming it. Ask yourself, "Is this anger, disappointment, frustration, or something else?" Remember, we often experience a blend of emotions, so don't be afraid to label multiple feelings. Feeling scared? What specifically are you afraid of? Digging deeper into the *why* behind our emotions empowers us to then address the root cause and eventually, share these feelings with others in a healthy way.

We should also accept that our minds love filling in the blanks, especially about other people's behavior. So, when we're feeling rejected because we haven't heard from a family member, instead of jumping to conclusions, we should control how those blanks are filled in. Maybe they're swamped or unwell, not indifferent. Shonna Waters of BetterUp has popularized the compassionate technique of adding "just like me" to anything we blame others for. Imagine the other person (because there's usually someone else involved) dealing with the same human flaws you do. This simple reminder can help you consider alternative explanations and avoid jumping to negative conclusions that trigger unhealthy emotions.

**We Have Something to Say in How We Respond**

We're not at the mercy of our emotions, even though it sometimes feels a lot like we are. More often than not, we have a choice in how we react. Imagine your go-to response to anger is lashing out and that by choosing that response, you might damage your relationships and this might leave you feeling worse later. The next time anger flares, recognize you have a choice. Instead of exploding, could you try expressing your frustration in a non–combative way? Explore alternative responses and notice how they feel. How did the other person react? You might be surprised at the positive outcomes of a more mindful, empathetic, and self–compassionate approach.

**All Emotions Are Valid!**

It's absolutely okay to feel! Emotions are a normal response to life's experiences, so instead of judging ourselves for feeling angry or scared, we should acknowledge their validity. Let's practice more self-compassion, be kinder to ourselves, and recognize that these emotions are simply part of being human. Acceptance might feel like a small step, but it's a great leap toward managing our emotional state in a healthy way.

## The Impact of Unmanaged Emotions on Communication

Have you ever noticed how, when we're feeling proud, angry, or upset, our voices might rise, we might use big words, or even interrupt others? Similarly, when we're feeling insecure, afraid, or small, we might speak softly, avoid eye contact, or stick to one-sided conversations to avoid being interrupted. Our emotions dictate a lot of our behavior, but when they're unmanaged, they seem to have an even stronger pull on our behavior than we do. Our emotions are powerful forces that significantly impact our communication, especially in close relationships, where unmanaged emotions can lead to misunderstandings, hurt feelings, and even relationship ruptures.

Just as dangerous for a relationship are unacknowledged emotions. If we give it some time, we'll notice that many arguments between couples boil down to a few fundamental anxieties: Am I truly seen and valued? Do I have a say in this relationship? Can I count on my partner to be there for me? Ironically, these three questions answer most of those couple fights that seem meaningless in retrospect or from the outside.

When our emotional life is a messy indescribable soup of feelings, our communication is the same. How could we assertively express a need or a boundary when it is buried under too many layers to acknowledge? Communication is already a delicate dance, and when unmanaged or unacknowledged emotions enter the picture, things can get even messier. Clear communication requires clear communicators. Unfortunately, when our thoughts and feelings are a tangled mess, our communication style suffers, and we risk saying things that are difficult to take back. Unresolved emotional pain, like past hurts, anxieties, or insecurities, can lurk beneath the surface and act like emotional landmines, ready to explode at any moment.

Overwhelmed by these intense emotions, we can resort to unhealthy communication tactics such as sarcasm, gaslighting, stonewalling, attacking the character of the person instead of addressing the issue at hand, or simply employing hostility. These tactics might feel satisfying in the moment, but they aren't conducive to a healthy and truthful relationship.

It's clear that when we're trapped in an emotional whirlwind, communication suffers. When messy emotions hijack conversations, even minor issues turn explosive, so the key to clear communication is managing our emotions. By calming the emotional storm, we create space for our logical brain to step in. Only then can we truly hear our partner, use those communication techniques we're going to learn, and navigate challenges with the reason and respect they deserve.

## Journal Prompt

Sometimes it's tough to know what we're actually feeling, as we're quite adept at tricking ourselves and avoiding everything that might be uncomfortable. So, let's explore some questions to gain valuable insights into our, hopefully, mysterious but not quite mystifying emotional world:

- Can you name the emotion(s) you're experiencing right now?

- Where in your body can you feel this emotion?

- What message do you think this feeling is trying to tell you?

- Can you name what's holding you back from dealing with this?

For when you need a little help naming your emotions, download our more extensive list at www.modernflowcollective.com/freetools.

# Step 2: Understanding Your Partner

Chapter 4:
# Recognizing Your Own and Your Partner's Communication Style

Imagine trying to have a conversation in a language you don't understand a word of. Frustration, confusion, and missed messages are almost guaranteed. This is what communication in a relationship can feel like when you don't understand your own or your partner's style. Their needs and yours might inadvertently fall on deaf ears.

Just like a decoder helps you translate symbols into their true meaning, understanding your partner's style allows you to interpret their words and actions more accurately, and understand the past experiences that made them choose those exact ones. They might say a convincing "I'm fine," but their body language might tell a different story (crossed arms, furrowed brow). By being aware of their nonverbal cues or communication habits, you can see beyond the surface meaning and understand their true feelings.

## How to Identify Communication/Attachment Styles

It wouldn't be farfetched to say that communication is the lifeblood of any relationship. It lets us feel truly seen and understood by others, just as it allows us to truly see and understand our partner. However, as mentioned previously, the way we communicate is deeply linked to our attachment styles and all those early patterns formed in childhood, that still influence our adult relationships. In other words, the way we naturally communicate with our partner, and the way our partner communicates with us, can reveal a lot about how we both approach intimacy and connection.

Essentially, we all have a toolbox filled with communication styles: passive, aggressive, passive-aggressive, and assertive. These styles, shaped by both of our upbringings, influence how we get our messages across. While one communication style may come more naturally to our partner, some styles build stronger bonds than others. Understanding your partner's communication style allows you not just to understand them and adapt, but can also prevent misunderstandings and create a communication haven—a place where you both feel heard and respected.

**Passive Default Style**

Does your partner avoid eye contact and mumbles "Sure, whatever you like" when you suggest a movie night? That's a good glimpse into the world of passive communicators. They tend to be quiet and reserved, prioritizing harmony and people pleasing over expressing their own needs. Decisions are left to others and apologies flow freely.

While this peace-loving style keeps conflict at bay, it can also bury needs and leave passive communicators feeling unheard or even uncared for, which is quite common with someone who developed an anxious attachment style. It's not that they don't have an opinion or feeling, but even though they might simmer beneath the surface, the discomfort with confrontation keeps them from openly expressing their preference. In the long run, this emotional suppression can make it difficult to have their needs met in relationships.

**Aggressive Default Style**

Let's go back to the movie selection scenario. This is where the aggressive communicator will show their colors and will launch into a tirade about their dislike of your choices, using harsh words and a loud voice. People with this style prioritize getting their point across, often resorting to yelling, domineering the conversation, or speaking forcefully without considering the impact on others.

They might often come across as defensive or even hostile, prioritizing their needs at the expense of anyone else's feelings, even if that wasn't their intention. On the contrary, they might feel like they're being efficient, but this harsh approach alienates the listener and makes it difficult for a productive conversation to happen. Because of the one-sidedness of this communication style, the message gets lost in the delivery, often leading to bigger arguments or resentment.

## Passive–Aggressive Default Style

In the same movie scenario, one partner avoids saying they're unhappy about the movie choice, but then they make pointedly negative comments about the film throughout the night. This is passive-aggressive communication in a nutshell. These folks often have a disconnect between their true feelings and how they express them. On the surface, they might seem agreeable, but their hidden anger or frustration manifests in underhanded ways—sarcasm, silence, sulking, or procrastination.

They might not realize it, but such manipulative behavior leaves the other person confused and forced to decipher cryptic messages instead of having a clear conversation. It's a frustrating cycle for both parties—the passive-aggressive person feels unheard, and the recipient is left feeling just as confused and unheard, a similar situation to that of how the passive-aggressive communicator felt growing up and developed a disorganized attachment style.

## Assertive Default Style

This is the partner who most likely developed a secure attachment style and who confidently shares their movie preferences, directly stating their desires, while also acknowledging others' suggestions. It's the sweet spot, balancing emotional honesty with respect for others.

Assertive communicators express themselves clearly and directly, avoiding hidden meanings or aggressive tactics. They can say *no* politely, and they feel comfortable sharing both their needs and their opinions. This open and honest style fosters healthy dialogue, reducing conflict and stress for everyone involved. Assertive communicators might not always get their way, but they get their message across clearly and respectfully. It's a win-win—they feel heard, and the other person feels valued.

While the assertive communication style is the gold standard, it's okay if your partner, or you for that matter, fall into another category. Just be mindful of your individual styles and observe how you both express yourselves and if the messages are being heard effectively, harshly, coming across like a double-edged sword, or not being heard at all.

## Common Misunderstandings Between Different Styles

Let's use an example: You and your partner are trying to plan a vacation. You, an assertive communicator, clearly state your desire for a relaxing beach getaway. Your partner, on the other hand, leans towards a passive style, offering vague suggestions but never truly voicing their preference for an adventurous mountain trip. This mismatch in communication styles can be a recipe for misunderstandings and frustration. They don't get their needs met, or their voice heard, and you don't understand what went wrong.

Communication styles also significantly impact emotional intimacy. Assertive communication, where both partners feel safe expressing needs and feelings, fosters trust and connection, but passive-aggressive tactics, like silent treatment or backhanded compliments, can create confusion and mistrust. The good news is that by understanding your own communication style and your partner's, you can bridge the gap. Recognizing these styles and making a conscious effort to be more assertive for yourself and to counteract your partner's communication style, can lead to a more fulfilling and emotionally connected relationship. So, next time you're planning a vacation (or anything else), take a moment to consider your communication styles and strive for a more open and honest dialogue.

**Passive and Assertive**

Social anxiety and low confidence can trap someone in a cycle of passive communication, where they hold back from expressing their needs and wants. This leads to unmet needs, fueling their anxiety and making it even harder to speak up. However, an assertive communicator can be their best guide. By confidently expressing your thoughts and feelings while insisting on discovering and respecting their needs, you create an environment where social anxiety and low confidence can be gradually chipped away.

## Aggressive and Assertive

Someone who talks over you, uses blame ("It's all your fault!"), and prioritizes winning arguments at all costs is an aggressive communicator, a style often employed by bullies and narcissists, but one that can creep into anyone's conversations. It leaves the other person feeling attacked and undermines relationships. Phrases like "My way or the highway" highlight the aggressive focus on dominance, and the intense and confrontational tone can be exhausting and frightening.

This is where an assertive communicator comes in, moderating the aggressive one. Assertiveness is a powerful tool when dealing with aggression. Both styles are about expressing their own needs, but assertive communication scores high on respecting others' needs as well. Instead of blaming or yelling, assertiveness uses "I" statements ("I feel frustrated") and focuses on finding solutions that work for everyone ("How can we compromise?"). Assertiveness builds relationships, while aggression damages them because it fails to take into account different sets of needs and perspectives.

## Passive-Aggressive and Assertive

If you're already an assertive communicator, or at least strive to be, yet you're still feeling unheard, you may be in a conversation with a master of the passive-aggressive communication style. This means they express negativity indirectly, through sighs, sarcasm, or even sulking, rather than directly voicing their needs. Often unaware of the impact, they might believe the world isn't receptive to their feelings. This frustration, fear, or resentment fuels their indirect communication.

For assertive communicators, this can be confusing, and all those mixed messages layered with a lack of trust can cloud conversations significantly. Having the passive-aggressive communicator leave their guard down can be a tough job as they might have grown up in environments where expressing emotions directly leads to shame or punishment, but it is possible. Acknowledge their feelings, offer a chance to talk openly, and gently guide them toward a more direct communication style where speaking your mind isn't met with severe repercussions.

Whenever another mix of communication styles is at play, and not one where at least one of the parties is an assertive communicator, misinterpretations can run rampant, as both sides struggle to understand the other's underlying feelings. Assertive communicators are the "communication chameleons" of relationships. When you're confident enough to express yourself clearly, you can also adapt your style to support a passive partner or counter an aggressive or passive-aggressive one. This win-win approach, where both of you feel heard and respected, is key for a healthy relationship. Even if your partner isn't naturally assertive, leading by example, you can inspire them to adopt a more confident and collaborative communication style.

## Adapting Your Communication to Suit Your Partner's Style

Disagreements happen in all relationships, but thriving couples are those who can repair the damage afterwards. Any couple, even healthy ones, yell and fight sometimes simply because our childhood experiences have inadvertently shaped how we handle conflict. These past patterns might flare up during stressful moments, but the good news is that you can learn from these fights and use them to strengthen your bond. Every time you make-up, you lessen negativity and build trust, and this helps you heal as a couple.

However, since you're reading this book, I must assume that you're interested to figure out your communication style and hopefully, transform it into the most effective of them all—the assertive one. Gladly, this communication style offers you the most flexibility and ability to connect, regardless of your partner's communication style. You can adapt any other communication styles, understand your partner's underlying needs, and work with them to reframe, dare to say more, or evolve what has been their natural communication style until then.

### Your Partner Is a Passive Communicator

People pleasing, a common result and cause of passive communication, may seem helpful at first. However, your partner's desire to appease everyone can lead them to overwhelm themselves. Often lacking confidence, they shy away from voicing their opinions and take a backseat in discussions. This submissive style, while sometimes mistaken for easygoingness, is often a way to avoid conflict. The real issue here is that passive communicators bottle up their needs, leading to resentment and ultimately hindering connection.

How to encourage communication:

- Ditch the pushy "be more confident" talk and instead, focus on building them up with genuine compliments, regardless if you compliment them on their effort or results. This fosters confidence in a supportive way.

- There's no space for anger or aggression. It shuts them down completely, and their low confidence crumbles under forceful approaches.

- Since shyness reigns supreme with them, cut through the silence by directly asking for their thoughts. This shows genuine interest and creates space for them to contribute, boosting their confidence.

- Resist shutting down their ideas even if you're convinced they won't work. Instead, highlight the positive aspects (e.g., "Interesting perspective!") and collaborate on finding alternative solutions that work for both of you. This builds trust and encourages them to contribute more and thus, increase their confidence.

**Your Partner Is an Aggressive Communicator**

Aggressive communicators can unknowingly wreak havoc on relationship collaboration. They ooze hostility, dominate conversations, and fixate on winning at all costs. Their apparent self-importance leaves you feeling steamrolled and belittled, but they lack the self-awareness to recognize their abrasiveness, mistaking their style for a bold one.

How to inspire communication:

- They can be a communication minefield. Prepare for a tough conversation, take a deep breath, and approach the situation with patience before diving in.

- Address their communication style constructively. Avoid insults or harshness, instead, introduce positive communication styles and suggest specific changes. Highlight the benefits of calmer approaches, like improved trust and connection.

- For smooth sailing when they fall into their aggressive tendencies, keep conversations brief and focused. If they veer off-topic, gently redirect them to avoid getting tangled in unproductive territory.

- While some couples benefit from open communication, if your partner gets aggressive during discussions, consider taking a step back. Try written communication methods like texts or emails that give you time to collect your thoughts, respond calmly, and avoid escalating the situation in the heat of the moment.

**Your Partner Is a Passive-Aggressive Communicator**

This style of communicator hides aggression with a smile. While they may not yell, their veiled hostility can be just as damaging to a relationship as open aggression. Their sharp comments may come in the form of sarcasm and patronization, which can be incredibly hurtful to the receiver. It's important to recognize that this style of communication, while on the surface is harsh, has evolved as a means of protection for your partner. They may lack the confidence to be assertive and the skills to manage their emotions effectively. This again is a learned social skill like many others.

How to build up their confidence, while keeping aggression tendencies at bay:

- Similar to how you'd adapt to an aggressive communication style, resist the urge to retaliate! Engaging in a tit-for-tat fight only fuels the negativity, so instead, take a deep breath and try to address the underlying issues calmly.

- Ditch the blame game and focus on building them up. Be clear and positive in your communication and focus on offering solutions that benefit both of you. Also, remember their passive and lacking in confidence side and highlight the strengths they bring to the relationship.

- Instead of settling for cryptic comments or gossip, try a direct approach with your partner. Help them express themselves clearly and positively and take what they're trying to say, and rephrase it in a way that's assertive yet kind.

- Instead of getting caught up in their negativity, try to understand what's driving their passive-aggressive behavior. Is stress at work causing them to lash out indirectly? Are there unaddressed issues at home spilling over? Look for patterns—does their negativity peak before deadlines or after certain interactions? By figuring out the root cause, you can offer support and encourage them to communicate more openly and constructively.

You might be a confident communicator who can adapt, but that doesn't mean mirroring their unhealthy style or getting dragged down to their level. Stooping to passive, aggressive, or passive-aggressive styles just fuels the fire. Stay strong and calm in your assertive communication, and be confident that it's more effective to address the issue directly and peacefully, building a bridge to understanding rather than burning one with negativity.

## Journal Prompt

Adapting your communication style to your partner's in order to bring out the best in your relationship is a constant push and pull, while always keeping your goals in mind.

- How would you describe your communication style?

- Are there times when you and your partner misunderstand each other? Why might this be?

- What are some ways you could both work toward more effective communication styles?

## Chapter 5:
# Empathy and Active Listening

When we invite empathy and active listening into our romantic relationship, we gain the ability to put ourselves in our partner's shoes and experience the world from their perspective. It's about understanding not just their words, but also their emotions and the reasons behind them.

## The Importance of Empathy in Relationships

Moving beyond our own perspective and truly understanding our partner's emotional state and perspective allows us to validate each other's emotions, creating a sense of security and trust within the relationship. However, even though feeling what our partner is feeling might be second nature to us, and we might even understand those feelings, not all of us know what to do about it. To be able to get a more nuanced understanding, it's important to acknowledge that while "empathy" is often used as a broad term, there are actually three distinct types of empathy:

- **Affective empathy:** This describes our ability to not only understand someone's emotions, but also feel them ourselves. This can manifest as concern for their well-being, or even mirroring their emotional state—feeling happy when they're happy, or sad when they're sad.

- **Somatic empathy:** The feeling in our own body, all the physical sensations we experience in response to another's emotions, is how this type of empathy manifests. Witnessing someone's embarrassment might cause us to blush ourselves, or their anxiety could lead to a tightness in our own chest.

- **Cognitive empathy:** This focuses on the mental aspect, allowing us to understand what another person is thinking and feeling based on the situation. It's like having a window into their mind, helping us see things from their perspective and interpret their thoughts and motivations. Psychologists refer to this skill as theory of mind—the ability to understand that others have their own unique thoughts and feelings, and interpret them (Schaafsma et al., 2014).

Empathy acts as the social glue that strengthens all of our relationships. By understanding the thoughts and feelings of others, we can navigate social situations with greater ease. When we're having a conversation with our partner, we can either say things as we prefer to hear them, or we can tailor our responses to resonate and be better understood by our partner. Empathy allows us to do the second, and it's an invaluable asset in fostering a sense of connection and mutual understanding. Research even shows that strong social connections are vital for both physical and mental health. Having a supportive network— and we're undoubtedly the strongest pillars in our partners—can lower stress, boost happiness, and even improve our physical health (Harandi et al., 2017). Empathy is what consolidates this network, creating a foundation for strong, lasting relationships.

Even more, empathy isn't just about understanding; it compels us to act. When we see someone struggling, our empathy can trigger a desire to help, and this works both ways. We're more likely to lend a hand when we connect with someone's emotions, and others are more likely to help us when they feel empathy too. Research backs this up, showing empathy as a driving force behind this prosocial behavior (Decety et al., 2016). It allows us to recognize needs, understand distress, and motivates us to ease someone's suffering. Of course, this extends to our closest relationships.

While many empathy studies were done on siblings (Lam et al., 2012), many of us can attest to the fact that not only does higher empathy lead to less conflict and more warmth, but in romantic relationships, empathy also strengthens our ability to forgive (Kimmes & Durtschi, 2016).

The good news is that empathy isn't a fixed trait; it's a skill we can all develop, even if our attachment style has "taught" us that empathizing isn't safe for us. The best way to start practicing and building our empathy muscle is by actively listening to our partner.

## Techniques for Active Listening

Active listening is a communication skill that highlights being silent more than talking. It goes beyond just hearing the words spoken; active listening is about truly understanding the deeper meaning and intention behind what our partner is saying. This happens when we fully focus on them, processing their message, and seeking their perspective. This is about showing we're willing to be present, listen with empathy, and understand their situation and perspective, not just ours. Our partner doesn't only feel heard when we actively listen to them, but doing so strengthens our bond significantly.

### Immerse Yourself in the Conversation

Active listening isn't just about hearing the words; it's about being completely present in the moment. Think of it as stepping into your partner's world for a moment to truly understand their perspective by giving them your full attention with all your senses—sight, sound, and even a sense of their emotions. Don't let yourself be captured by your own thoughts or other distractions. To achieve this, put away your phone, silence any inner chatter, and focus solely on your partner. By letting go of everything else, you create a space for deeper connection and understanding.

### Body Language Says What Words Couldn't

Considering that communication is more than stringing words together, active listening is about picking up non-verbal cues too. Body language, facial expressions, and even tone of voice can reveal hidden emotions. A rapid pace might hint at nervousness, while slow speech could indicate tiredness or careful consideration. Remember, you're sending messages too, so if you'd like your partner to truly open up, maintain open body language, avoid crossing your arms, and offer a warm smile to show genuine engagement.

## The Right Amount of Eye Contact Builds Bridges

This is one of the ways you can demonstrate that you're actively listening to your partner. However, avoid an intense stare that many of us perceive as threatening rather than as a show of openness. Aim for the 50/70 rule—make eye contact for 50-70% of the time they're speaking, holding it for 4-5 seconds before glancing away briefly (Schulz, 2012). This conveys attentiveness without making them feel uncomfortable or under scrutiny.

## Open–Ended Questions Drive Conversation

Active listening thrives on open-ended questions that spark conversation and deeper understanding. Instead of eliciting one-word answers such as *yes* and *no*, these questions encourage your partner to elaborate and share their perspective. Examples include: "Can you tell me more about that?" or "What do you think is the best way forward?" Not only do these open-ended questions show genuine curiosity and encourage those who aren't always comfortable to speak their minds, but they also make your partner feel valued.

## Patience Is Never Overrated

Patience is the bedrock of active listening as it allows your partner the space to fully express themselves without feeling rushed or interrupted. Resist the urge to fill silences with your own thoughts or stories. Remember, the goal is to understand, not simply respond. Don't formulate a reply in your head while they're still speaking, and avoid abruptly changing the subject—this can signal boredom and a lack of interest. Allow them to set the pace of conversation.

## Judgment Doesn't Get a Seat at This Table

During active listening, you transform yourself into a supportive sounding board, so withholding judgment is crucial. It's okay not to agree with your partner, but now isn't the moment to express that. Now it's their time to open up and your responsibly to help them get there. By remaining neutral and non-critical, you create a safe space for your partner to express themselves openly. They should feel comfortable sharing their thoughts without fear of shame, blame, or negativity.

Our brains are wired to make quick judgments, but in active listening, it's crucial to catch ourselves before reacting negatively. Once we recognize these signs, it's time to redirect our thoughts toward understanding. Our priority here is to stay curious and not to label our partner in any way, but sometimes, even with good intentions, miscommunication happens. Don't be afraid to ask for clarification when you don't quite understand something they referred to. Asking rather than assuming prevents misunderstandings and ensures you're truly on the same page.

## How to Validate Your Partner's Feelings and Experiences

Emotional validation isn't about suppressing negativity; it's about creating a safe space for all emotions. It allows our partner to fully experience their feelings, both positive and negative, and acknowledge their validity. This can be especially helpful when they're struggling with difficult emotions, as it shows we understand and accept them even as they are in that moment.

Finger-pointing, whether at ourselves or our partner, is a common but ineffective tactic during conflict because it backfires by creating a blame game and only hinders resolution or emotional validation. Australian coach James "Fish" Gill has a great saying about fixing relationship issues: "If someone has to be wrong in repair, then it's not repair" (2024).

Another trap we might have fallen into is, instead of accepting and validating our partner's emotions, we're trying to cheer them up with forced positivity. While positive thinking has its place, overdoing it can lead to toxic positivity and this can actually harm our partner's mental health. When we're forcing positivity onto them, we're essentially invalidating their feelings. The right kind of emotional validation happens only when we truly understand and accept their feelings, even if they're negative.

## Offering Comfort Isn't the Same as Support

Our first instinct when someone shares a tough situation, or when we face bad news ourselves, is to offer immediate comfort. Phrases like "everything will be fine in the end" or "there's a silver lining to everything" tumble out, driven by our desire to help. However, these might not be what our partner needs. Rather, pause and reflect before responding. This initial step of pausing gives us the time to understand our own emotional responses and decide not to react to them, but prioritize our partner so we can better understand and validate their feelings.

## Putting a Name to Feelings

After truly listening to your partner's situation and resisting the urge to gloss over their feelings with forced positivity, the next step is acknowledging their emotions. Phrases like "I understand you're feeling really sad" or "That sounds incredibly frustrating" go a long way. Don't downplay their emotions or try to minimize the situation. By validating their feelings, you show them you hear them and care about their experience. This empathetic response creates a safe space for them to express themselves freely and begin processing their emotions.

## Assumptions and Unsolicited Advice Are off the Table

Not only is it unhealthy, but there's no point in dictating emotions or telling our partner how we think they "should" feel. Rather, were better off letting them know it's okay to express their true feelings, both positive and negative. Moreover, we should acknowledge their vulnerability and the courage it takes to be open and honest. Phrases like "I appreciate you sharing your true feelings" or "It takes strength to be this open" validate their emotional experience and show you value their honesty.

## Validation, Validation, Validation

True and healthy communication only happens in the presence of validation. Don't try to fix your partner's emotions, but rather accept them and express your acceptance with phrases such as "That sounds really difficult" or "I can see why you'd feel that way." Validation shows you understand and care about them.

You can also offer simple support, like "I'm here for you" or "Let me know how I can help." Remember, you're both allowed to feel your emotions, so don't forget to acknowledge your own challenges and remind each other that difficult feelings are temporary. By allowing yourself to feel them, you can both move through the situation in a healthier way. As so many therapists like to say: The only way past emotions is through them (Gill, 2024).

# Journal Prompt

Before we get into this chapter's journal prompt, please remember that empathy, like any trait of ours, is something we can improve upon with practice. So, if you're curious how empathetic you are naturally, let's get to journaling:

- Do people feel comfortable confiding in you?

- Do you pick up on subtle cues about how people are truly feeling?

- Can you think of a situation when you took time to think about how your actions might affect others emotionally?

# Step 3:
# Effective Communication Techniques

Chapter 6:
# The Art of Conversation

Conversation in a romantic relationship is a two-way street of small talk, deep talk, sharing dreams, emotions, opinions, vulnerability, and strengths. It's revealing ourselves layer by layer and witnessing our loved ones reveal themselves in turn. When we support each other to share our deepest thoughts and feelings, we become more resilient in the face of challenge and change; we become able to laugh at life's little ironies and be in awe at its beauty. We exchange little pieces of ourselves, and the "I" we were before creating this connection becomes a different "I," one more synonymous with "we," but without compromising our identities. All of this, simply by employing the art of conversation.

## Starting and Maintaining Meaningful Conversations

While some may be naturally gifted conversationalists, anyone can learn to initiate engaging discussions in a romantic relationship. The key lies in moving beyond small talk. Sure, discussing the weather or the latest news can be a starting point, but it rarely sparks a deeper connection. It is when we focus on conversations that ignite curiosity and emotional engagement that the real spark happens.

### Initiating More Than Small Talk

To make sure you kick things off right, you'd normally look for any common ground, but since this is your partner and you already know what that common ground entails, consider changing things up and tailoring your approach to your partner's interests. Do they love history? Ask about a recent documentary they might have enjoyed. Are they passionate about music? Discuss a new band or upcoming concert. Another great conversation starter that goes beyond warming up your vocal cords with small talk is asking for advice. Of course, this can sometimes involve revealing insecurities or uncertainties, but your partner's supportive response can create a safe space for open communication and emotional intimacy. The initial question about advice can easily lead to more in-depth discussions, and their response might reveal their own values, experiences, or ways of approaching similar situations.

## Maintaining Great Conversations

I mentioned open–ended questions in the previous chapter as the well–oiled motor driving conversation, but they are what keeps the *meaningful* conversation going as well. Instead of "Did you have a good day?" try "What was the highlight of your day?" These "why," "how," and "what" questions encourage them to elaborate, share their thoughts and feelings, and will make the conversation more interesting for both of you. While open-ended questions can help you get information, the key is to be authentic. Don't manipulate the conversation to get something specific, but rather focus on genuine curiosity and a desire to understand your partner better, and simply go with the flow of conversation.

I appreciate that these aren't questions for everyday conversation, but when the timing seems right, consider asking your partner some of these questions, and maybe even extend yourself the same and journal about them:

- If there were no physical or financial limitations, what secret dream would you always hold close to your heart? How could we make it a reality together?

- I'd love to spend some quality time with you tomorrow. Is there anything you'd especially enjoy doing together?

- If you could have a wide reach and influence the world, what kind of impact would you want to make? Would recognition help you achieve that?

- If you could have a one-on-one conversation with any historical figure, who would it be and why? What specific questions would you have for them?

- If you could live anywhere in the world and be as connected as you are now to friends and family, where would you live and why?

While great conversations are a lot about asking or being asked the right questions, the key lies in truly listening to what our conversation partner is saying. Paying attention to keywords, phrases, or even the emotions they express, we can use this knowledge as our springboard for more thoughtful questions. However, we must also remember that sometimes, comfortable silences are natural pauses in conversation. Don't feel pressured to fill every gap with immediate questions; just let the conversation breathe and allow your partner to elaborate if they wish. Conversations are collaboration and communion of minds, so it's only natural that at different times, both of you will be speaking or listening, but pausing to consider is just as indispensable to meaningful conversations.

## Balancing Speaking and Listening

Listening might sound simple enough, but it's a subtle balancing act. We actively take in information while showing we care and we're not passive, just waiting for our turn to talk. This attentive focus shapes conversations as much as our words would. Actively showing we're engaged validates our partner's experience and vulnerability. Whether it's a story, a struggle, or a dream, the true connection comes from a balance of thoughtful speaking and deep listening. After all, our human need to belong is met through shared experiences. We all crave being heard, just as much as we have a desire to connect with others through our own stories.

It's no surprise that the cornerstone of strong relationships is the ability to truly listen. While talking can be fun and necessary, genuine listening is often the more crucial ingredient, and the one that doesn't always come easily. However, there's a catch to listening. Instead of mentally crafting a response, actively absorb your partner's thoughts and feelings. This shift from listening to react to listening to learn is the first step to stronger communication and a deeper connection.

Communication in a relationship is a beautiful dance with two essential roles: the talker and the listener. While mastering both is crucial, ensuring everyone gets a chance to shine is key. The ability to express ourselves openly and honestly is vital, but expressing ourselves is only half the story. Being truly listened to, with our partner actively engaged and present, validates our experiences, and we want to do the same for them. A good rule of thumb is that when our partner is talking, we should give them our full attention. Make eye contact, nod occasionally if everything is clear or ask clarifying questions, and avoid interrupting.

Instead of one partner dominating the conversation, we should take turns. After expressing ourselves, let's invite our partner to share their thoughts and feelings. When we feel heard and understood, and our partner feels the same, this back-and-forth exchange strengthens the foundation of our relationship and allows love to blossom.

However, since not all moments are created equal for those deep and meaningful talks we all crave, it's certainly not a great time to bring up a heavy topic when our partner is busy out of their mind, stressed, or already having a tough day. If this is not the case but you're still not quite sure if it's a great time for a conversation, a simple "Is this a good time to talk?" shows respect and sets the stage for a more productive conversation.

All in all, mastering the art of balancing listening and talking takes practice! A good starting point is to become a better listener in your relationship by being fully present when your partner is doing the talking. Put away distractions, make eye contact, and use your body language to show you're engaged. Actively listen by paraphrasing what you hear to confirm understanding. Most importantly, step into their shoes and try to see things from their perspective. This combination of focus, confirmation, and empathy builds trust and strengthens your connection, but when reciprocity is involved, when your partner does the same for you, it is when a deep and sustainable connection happens.

## Navigating Small Talk and Deep Conversations

Small talk and long, meaningful conversations are both part of a healthy couple's life. They both have the proper place and time.

Being a master at small talk is a valuable skill to have in life, and who better to practice this skill with than your partner? Anyone can become a conversation pro with the right mindset, especially when that is a growth mindset. Unlike a fixed mindset that believes skills are set in stone, a growth mindset embraces the power of practice. It essentially allows you to step outside your comfort zone without feeling discouraged. Every conversation, even the seemingly awkward ones, becomes a chance to learn and improve. The good thing is that small talk doesn't have to be about the weather. Choose a light subject of your liking and initiate the conversation. Small talk thrives on safe topics. Skip sensitive areas like politics, religion, or finances, for now, and flip through great alternatives that include entertainment (movies, books), art, sports, travel, and, if nothing else comes to mind, even the weather.

Small talk serves a purpose, keeping the conversation flowing and easing social interactions or even easing you into a more complex conversation with your partner. But it's only natural that sometimes, we crave something deeper. Meaningful conversations, or as researcher Mehl and his team coined them, "substantive," go beyond the surface-level pleasantries (Milek et al., 2018). The key ingredient in a meaningful conversation is learning. These conversations spark curiosity, where you exchange information and gain new perspectives. Sure, you might learn from a repair service professional or a doctor's visit, but meaningful conversations go beyond that. They allow you to gain a deeper understanding of yourself, the other person, or the world around you. These are the conversations that truly connect us and leave a lasting impact.

While the most straightforward way to transition from small talk to a substantive conversation is by asking open–ended questions, meaningful conversations aren't just information exchanges between partners; they're journeys of self-discovery. Unlike monologues or journaling, a good listener is essential. Through their attentive presence, they reflect back who we are, offering valuable feedback. We see ourselves through their eyes. This cycle of speaking, listening, and self-reflection fosters connection, the final piece of the puzzle.

It's clear that having a meaningful conversation is more taxing than having small talk for most of us, so you might ask yourself why you should go through all the trouble? The same group of researchers that called meaningful conversations "substantive" found that people with richer conversations report higher life satisfaction. While it's unclear if meaningful talks cause happiness or happy people just talk more deeply, the connection between the two is undeniable. Ultimately, feeling understood and connected is a recipe for well-being (Milek et al., 2018).

Meaningful conversations fulfill a basic human need: to feel connected. We learn not just about ourselves, but also about our partner and the world around us. The result, as expected, is a deeper understanding and a stronger sense of belonging, which, it turns out, also makes us feel happier.

## Journal Prompt

Another aspect of the same study mentioned above, which immediately caught my attention, is that deep thinkers, those who spend time contemplating life's bigger meanings, are more likely to engage and enjoy a conversation that goes beyond the basics (Milek et al., 2018). So, to get some practice at having more meaningful conversations, let's open our minds to meaningful subjects in the comfort of our journal first:

- If you could wake up every day with a guaranteed chance to pursue something you're truly passionate about, what would that be?

- Have you faced any challenging situations in the past that might have left you feeling afraid or cautious?

- What internal sense of accomplishment or fulfillment would make you feel truly successful?

# Chapter 7:
# Nonverbal Communication

While until now we focused more on what and when to say something, communication isn't just about what we say, but also how we and our bodies say it. Nonverbal communication, an intrinsic communication element according to the American Psychological Association, conveys information through a variety of silent cues (2018). Facial expressions, hand gestures, eye contact, and even physical distance or closeness all play a role in shaping our message. A raised eyebrow can be a conversation breaker, a warm smile can put someone at ease, and crossed arms might signal a closed mind. By understanding nonverbal communication and syncing it with our words, we can ensure our message lands as intended.

## The Power of Body Language, Tone, and Facial Expressions

Believe it or not, the bulk of our message isn't carried by words. Studies suggest nonverbal communication reigns supreme, with some estimating it makes up 80% of what we convey (Hull, 2016). Think about it: postures, facial expressions, eye contact, gestures, and even the tone of our voice all speak volumes. Every day, we're bombarded with these silent cues, from a firm handshake to a nervous fidget. This nonverbal language is a window into who we are, shaping how we connect with others.

### Facial Expressions

Our faces are louder than we think they are! Facial expressions play a major role in nonverbal communication and it's often the first thing we notice about someone, even before their words register. Interestingly, while cultures can influence nonverbal communication styles, some facial expressions seem universal.

Paul Ekman, a renowned psychologist, embarked on groundbreaking research to explore the universality of facial expressions. He ventured to remote cultures with minimal exposure to Western media. By studying people's reactions to staged emotional scenarios, Ekman initially identified strong evidence for seven basic emotions—happiness, sadness, anger, surprise, contempt, disgust, and fear—being expressed and recognized universally through facial expressions. This research challenged the notion that emotions are purely cultural and suggested a biological basis for these core expressions (Eckman, 1999).

**Gestures**

Hand and body gestures are like another language, adding meaning to our communication without uttering a sound. From a friendly wave to a thumbs-up, some gestures are universally understood, but we should also watch out because, unlike facial expressions, gestures can also be culturally specific.

This power of nonverbal communication extends to public speakers, politicians, and even courtrooms, where judges may limit gestures to prevent swaying the jury. A subtle glance at a watch or an eye roll can send strong messages about the perceived importance of someone's words, so these are not gestures we'll need in our arsenal when engaged in active listening.

**Paralinguistics**

Another superpower often employed by politicians, but something we also do more or less unconsciously, is paralinguistics. This is all about *how* we say the words, including elements like tone, volume, inflection, and pitch. Think about how a simple "okay" can sound enthusiastic or completely bored, depending on how you say it.

Paralinguistics are powerful tools that can completely change the meaning of what you're trying to convey. A strong, confident tone might be interpreted as approval, while a hesitant whisper could signal disinterest or lack of confidence. Instead of reading between the lines, we read between the words to better understand if there's a more subtle message being conveyed.

## Posture and Body Language

While much of our posture and movements are habits, they're communication tools too. Body language research has boomed since the 70s, but the more it's studied, the more it appears that it's not always as clear-cut as some popular media portrays it. While crossed arms *can* signal defensiveness, it's not always the case. Body language is often subtle and open to interpretation. A confident posture might project authority, but a slouch could also indicate someone's being comfortable and relaxed. The key takeaway is that body language and posture are important pieces of the puzzle, but they're best understood in context alongside other nonverbal cues.

## Physical Closeness

Ever feel like someone was standing a bit too close for your comfort, or maybe, on the contrary, you craved a friendly hug? Welcome to the world of proxemics, the study of personal space. This invisible bubble surrounding us is a form of nonverbal communication, but how much space we need, and what we consider *ours*, depends on a variety of factors. Culture, social norms, the situation, and even our personalities, all play a role. A casual conversation might happen within 18 inches to 4 feet (46 cm to 1.2 m), but the closer we feel to the person, the smaller this space becomes.

## Eye Gaze

From simple glances to intense stares, eye gaze speaks volumes. Have you ever noticed your blink rate increase when you see something you like? That's nonverbal communication in action! Our eyes can hint at a range of emotions, from interest to attraction, and even influence how trustworthy we appear. Steady eye contact often suggests honesty, while someone looking away might be perceived as deceptive. But, as with posture and body language, eye gaze isn't a foolproof lie detector, it's just one piece of the nonverbal puzzle.

While understanding nonverbal communication is a powerful tool that helps us convey information, reinforce meaning, and build trust, it's also a great ace up our sleeves when we observe our partner's subtle reactions. When we understand communication in its entirety, we can clarify our assumptions, and adapt to our partner's both the verbal and nonverbal cues.

## How to Read and Respond to Nonverbal Cues

While in our romantic relationships, we don't need the level of perceptiveness an interrogator has; we can still learn to notice slight shifts in our partner's body language. Pay attention to their posture, eye contact, facial expressions, and any habitual gestures they might have when they're relaxed and at ease. Do they act any differently now that your conversation subject might be challenging?

**Inconsistencies**

In a romantic relationship, this would translate to noticing when we're tackling a subject that makes our partner act in any way uncharacteristically. Pay attention to inconsistencies between spoken words and nonverbal communication. These inconsistencies can be subtle, but they can also be glaring, like our partner saying "yes" while shaking their head no. Similarly, a forced smile while delivering bad news might signal discomfort or hesitation, and lack of eye contact while saying "I'm listening" could indicate disinterest or something left unsaid. Crossed arms while offering help might convey a closed-off or guarded attitude, while a monotone voice while expressing excitement might sound unconvincing.

When this happens, it doesn't necessarily mean that our partner is lying. They could be nervous, uncomfortable with the topic, or simply not fully engaged in the conversation. However, they can be a red flag that something deeper is going on, something we can observe and clarify.

## Group All Nonverbal Signals in a Bundle

The most similar situation to this is when a conductor is leading an orchestra. Each instrument plays its own part, but the magic happens when they all come together in harmony. Nonverbal communication isn't about a single gesture or facial expression; it's about the entire body of nonverbal cues working together to create a message and the context they're in.

Pay attention to all the nonverbal signals you're receiving: eye contact, facial expressions, body language, posture, gestures, tone of voice, and even silence. Are the nonverbal cues reinforcing the spoken words, or is there a disconnect, an inconsistency? Is the subject sensitive, controversial, or is it small talk? Are they trying to cope with the overwhelming subject by taking up as little space as possible even though they are normally a confident person? Or are they avoiding eye contact and possibly avoiding the subject? Notice these cues and ask for clarifications in a compassionate way.

## Let Your Intuition Do Part of the Work

We've all experienced that gut feeling—a hunch that something isn't quite right, even if we can't pinpoint why. When it comes to nonverbal communication, this intuition can be a powerful tool. Our brains are constantly processing nonverbal cues, often on a subconscious level, and while we might not consciously register a fleeting change in facial expression without practice, our intuition might pick up on it.

When there's a disconnect between verbal and nonverbal communication, our intuition can trigger a red flag. Our partner saying "I'm fine" with a forced smile might set off our internal alarm because the words and body language don't align, but as mentioned before, let's not jump to conclusions just yet. Not every inconsistency means dishonesty, so we need to consider the situation and our partner's baseline behavior before asking clarifying questions to see if their feelings align with the nonverbal cues we're picking up on.

Remember, body language isn't an exact science, so reading nonverbal communication should be used in conjunction with conscious observation and critical thinking. But by trusting our guts and paying attention to nonverbal cues, we can become more effective communicators and navigate the world with greater confidence and understanding.

## Synchronizing Verbal and Nonverbal Messages

We could all benefit from speaking with our whole body more often. We all had a friend excitedly telling us about their holiday—their voice bubbles with energy, their eyes sparkle, and they might even gesture with excitement. That's the power of synchronized communication! It builds trust, makes us appear confident, and ensures our message is more crystal clear than the pool from our friend's holiday.

However, just like many other aspects pertaining to communication, starting with ourselves first, self–awareness, is the key to understanding and reading others.

### Put the Magnifying Glass on Your Behavior

Have you ever noticed your smile widen when you're truly happy, or your voice drop when you're feeling down? Our bodies are amazing storytellers, even before we speak a word! By paying attention to your own gestures, facial expressions, and tone of voice in different situations, we can unlock a treasure trove of self-discovery. This self-awareness will not only give us valuable insights into our emotions, but will also equip us to use nonverbal communication to our advantage in any situation.

### Gather the Puzzle Pieces of Your Partner's Baseline

We can all learn from watching others, and since our partner is closer to us, next time we're in a conversation, let's pay attention. What kind of stories do their faces tell? Are their gestures animated or subdued? By becoming a keen observer of nonverbal communication, we gain the ability to quickly pick up on how they might be feeling, even if they're trying to protect us from that information.

This skill can also be a source of inspiration. When you see someone you admire projecting confidence with their posture, remember the nonverbal cocktail they employed and add it to your own communication toolbox.

## Catch Yourself Before You Snap

We've all been there—the rude driver cuts you off, and before you know it, an uncharacteristic gesture flies out the window. While our reaction and what we feel would be 100% in sync, this is where we'd be better off pausing and breaking that link by changing these impulsive reactions. The key is to interrupt the pattern. Instead of letting our anger control your body language, we should train ourselves to pause and take a breath. This split second can make all the difference in keeping our cool when a conversation elicits the same reactions. When we lose our minds in this way, we lose our ability to read nonverbal cues.

## Give Your Partner the Benefit of the Doubt

Nonverbal communication is a powerful tool, but it's important to remember that it's not a universal language. A crossed arm in one culture might signal defensiveness, while in another, it could just be someone feeling cold. The same goes for tone of voice or facial expressions. Always seek clarification if your partner's body language seems off, and don't assume the worst. Instead, try something like, "Hey, I noticed you seem a bit quiet. Is everything okay?"

Our conversations aren't just about the words we say; they're a full-body experience. Nonverbal communication plays a huge role in how we get our message across and how we understand others. It's like looking at the whole picture of body expressions. By considering all these nonverbal cues alongside someone's spoken words, we can gain a deeper understanding of their true meaning and intentions, and act accordingly.

## Journal Prompt

Head out and observe someone you don't know. It could be anyone—at a coffee shop, walking down the street, waiting in line. Pay attention to the following aspects of their nonverbal communication:

- **Appearance:** Notice their overall look—hair style, clothing choices, any accessories.

- **Grooming:** How well-kept is their hair, clothing, and overall presentation?

- **General demeanor:** Are they relaxed and confident, tense and anxious, or somewhere in between?

- **Verbal behavior:** If they happen to be talking, listen for any clues in their tone of voice or word choice. (This might be limited depending on the situation.)

- **Social skills:** If they interact with anyone else, observe how they handle the interaction. Do they seem comfortable or awkward? Friendly or reserved?

Based on these nonverbal cues, form an impression of the person. What kind of mood are they in? What kind of personality might they have?

# Chapter 8:
# Conflict Resolution

Healthy disagreements are a normal part of any relationship, but navigating conflict in a romantic partnership, where we usually wear our hearts on our sleeve, can feel especially tricky. However, if there was one rule that could apply to any type of conflict, it's avoiding reactivity and, rather, looking beyond the immediate issue and trying to understand the underlying reasons for the conflict.

## Understanding the Role of Conflict in Relationships

While disagreements are inevitable in close relationships, a surprising perk emerges from research on conflict resolution: it can actually strengthen your bond! Experts have delved deep into communication and conflict, and discovered that healthy conflict, navigated with respect and understanding, can be a positive force (Caughlin et al., 2013).

### Signals That Change Is Needed

I believe, not many people could be accused of finding disagreements pleasant, but the surprising upside is that conflict can be a catalyst for positive change in our relationships. Think of it as a flashing red light, a signal that something needs attention. By addressing conflict constructively, both partners get a chance to voice concerns and work together toward solutions. This isn't just about patching things up; it's about identifying areas for growth and making our relationships stronger and more fulfilling in the long run. So, the next time a disagreement arises, remember—it could be an opportunity to create positive change, together.

## Shows That Your Lives Are Entwined

Relationships are a complex dance between partners. Sometimes, you'll be in perfect step, but other times, your movements might clash. However, this clash of the titans can actually strengthen your connection because conflict highlights your interdependence. Think about it—disagreements wouldn't exist if your lives weren't intertwined. Sharing a car, finances, or even just weekend plans creates a web of connection, but with connection comes the potential for occasional friction. The trick is not to let this simple conflict tear you apart, but instead become the team you need to be for navigating and enjoying the dance of life together.

## Grab Your Ice Pick and Get to the Core of Conflict

Disagreements can be like icebergs—the surface issue, that forgotten chore that was the catalyst, is just the tip. The real frustration often lies beneath, rooted in deeper feelings. Maybe that untaken trash bag represents a burden you silently carry, making you feel disrespected. Unearthing these hidden reasons is crucial for growth, but it's not always easy to appeal to ration in the heat of the moment. Here is where that invaluable cause between trigger and reaction comes in. Take a breath and cool down as much as possible. A calmer you is a more rational you. By addressing the core issues hidden beneath the surface, conflict becomes an opportunity. You can communicate your true feelings and work together on solutions, building a stronger, more understanding relationship.

# Strategies for Healthy Conflict Resolution

Many disagreements boil down to a lack of understanding; we get so focused on defending our point of view that we forget to listen to our partner's. Empathy is the secret weapon to turning conflicts on their head. By trying to understand not just what we're feeling, but what our partner is feeling as well and why this issue matters to them, we can start to untangle the knot.

What's really bothering you, and what might be going on for your partner? Even if they're not ready to delve deep just yet, you can take control of your own communication. Start by examining your own motivations and concerns. What are you hoping to achieve by addressing this issue? By understanding yourself better, you can communicate with more clarity and empathy, even if your partner isn't quite there yet. This shift in focus, from "me" to "we," can work wonders. Feeling truly understood can be incredibly validating, paving the way for a more productive conversation and a stronger bond.

Feeling understood after conflict is simply a balm. It shows our partner cares and is invested in working through the issue together. This reaffirms the strength of our bond and makes the relationship feel worth fighting for. Ultimately, being heard and understood, even when we disagree, is simply a powerful feel-good factor that strengthens our connection. Let's explore some ways in which we can turn down the volume, and turn up the understanding:

- **Step into their shoes, not onto their toes:** Instead of pushing your viewpoint, try walking a mile/ kilometer in your partner's shoes. Make understanding their feelings your top priority. What experiences or emotions might be driving their perspective?

- **Navigate in calmer waters:** Steer clear of the rocky shores of criticism, defensiveness, contempt, and stonewalling. Opt for more productive calm, and respectful communication.

- **Extend a hand, not an accusation:** Start by believing your partner has good intentions, even if you disagree. Offer them the benefit of the doubt and choose open communication over suspicion.

- **Rekindle the appreciation flame:** Before reacting, take a moment to reflect on the reasons you fell for your partner in the first place. Remember the qualities you value most about your partner, like a treasure you're grateful to have.

- **You and your partner are on the same side of the table, not across from it:** You're both working together to understand the issue and find a solution that works for everyone. You're not competitors; you're on the same team.

- **Maintaining calm can be tough:** Following these tips might not always be easy, especially if your partner isn't on the same page. But remember, even small efforts toward better communication can make a big difference.

Disagreements can trigger a firestorm of emotions, making it hard to think clearly, which is why we could all use the crutch of a mantra—short, powerful phrases we silently repeat to ourselves when anger starts to bubble up. Mantras redirect our attention away from the immediate frustration and toward our desired outcome. There's simply something about the rhythmic repetition of a calming phrase that can have a soothing effect on our nervous system, lowering your emotional temperature, and it can be as simple as "be understanding" or "understand before you react." But the best mantra is one that resonates with you, so rehearse it outside of conflict situations so it's readily available when you need it. However, if your initial mantra isn't working, try a different one that better reflects the situation.

Use any tool available to help you navigate conflict with more awareness and control. By using them consistently, you can transform heated moments into opportunities for growth and a stronger, understanding-driven relationship.

## Turning Conflicts Into Opportunities for Growth

Disagreeing doesn't have to mean defeat. Instead of trying to "win" or force your partner to see things your way, the best you can do is focus on understanding their perspective—seek common ground with empathy and curiosity. It's okay to feel emotions during conflict, but don't let them cloud your communication.

The secret weapon of relationship ninjas isn't that big of a secret to us anymore—active listening. One person speaks, the other truly listens, and then we switch. Remember, successful conflict resolution requires both sides to be engaged in this exchange of understanding. Half of conflict resolution is listening, and the other half is speaking.

**Being on the Listening Team**

Disagreements are rarely black and white, so instead of jumping to defend our position, we should listen with an open mind. Both of us have experiences that shape our view—two valid realities. So, let's try to hear the emotions behind our partner's words, even if the specifics are debatable. Put your own perspective on hold for a moment and see things from their side. Instead of demanding answers, let's unlock our partner's perspective with open-ended questions. Questions like "How does this make you feel?" or "What worries you most about this?" spark conversation and open their heart to share their experiences.

True listening goes beyond simply hearing words; it's about reflecting back on what we understand. Powerful listening involves summarizing our partner's perspective in our own words, ensuring we've captured their true feelings. This doesn't mean blind agreement—it's about acknowledging the validity of their experience with phrases like "I can see why you feel that way" or "It makes sense that you had those needs."

Validation, even of a small part of their position, helps build a bridge of understanding. Imagine negativity as a wall—by reflecting back on their emotions; we chip away at that wall. Lowered defenses and a feeling of being heard pave the way for navigating conflict with love, respect, and a deeper lasting connection.

**Being on the Speaking Team**

When it's our turn to speak, let's focus on clear communication that fosters understanding and, ideally, collaboration. Speak honestly about your feelings and beliefs on the issue, but avoid accusatory language. One trick that's often used in couple's therapy is the assumption of similarity—positive qualities you see in yourself likely exist in your partner too (Gottman & Gottman, 2015). Likewise, consider if negative traits you attribute to your partner might also be present in you to some degree. This shift in perspective can promote empathy and open the door to collaborative problem-solving. Remember, the goal is to work as a team toward solutions that address both your needs.

In the heat of disagreement, blaming and accusations fly freely, but these tactics rarely lead to solutions and often deepen the divide. That's where "I" statements come in—powerful tools that can transform conflict resolution. These types of statements shift the focus from attacking your partner to expressing your own experience and feelings. Instead of saying, "You never listen to me!", try "I feel like my opinion doesn't matter to you when you interrupt me." This approach is less accusatory and more likely to prompt empathy from your partner. By focusing on your feelings, you take responsibility for your emotional state, and this empowers you to find solutions rather than placing blame. When you express your feelings openly, you invite your partner to understand your perspective.

Most importantly, don't leave your partner guessing or worse, assuming, and clearly state your desires after hearing them out. The Gottman Method teaches that "within every complaint lies a longing" (Gottman & Gottman, 2015). By voicing that deeper need (the longing), you create a roadmap for finding solutions that fulfill both of you. Instead of focusing on the problem, shift the focus to what you both ultimately want—a stronger connection and a happier relationship.

Please remember that it is okay not to be perfect! These communication tips are tools, not tests, so even with stumbles, listening actively and speaking thoughtfully can keep your connection strong during conflict's emotional storms.

## Journal Prompt

Feeling accused triggers defensiveness, but "I" statements shift the focus to your own subjective experience. It's much healthier for both of you to use phrases such as "I feel frustrated when..." instead of "You always..."

Using the formula of "I feel [emotion] *when* [explanation]" reduces blame, it keeps you on the given issue without blowing it up to being about your own or your partner's character, and opens the door to finding solutions together.

Let's explore some scenarios and then the "I" statement equivalent, but if you feel inclined, add your own experiences to the list:

"You" statement: You work too much!

"I" statement: I've felt lonely this week without our usual dinners together.

"You" statement: You ghost me every time we're at a party!

"I" statement: I felt a little insecure when you were talking to someone else for a long time at the party. Did you have a good conversation?

"You" statement: You never care about me since you never call during the day.

"I" statement: I miss hearing from you throughout the day. Knowing you're thinking of me, even with a quick text, helps me feel connected.

# Step 4:
# Build Stronger Connections

Chapter 9:
# Building Trust and Intimacy

Comparing relationships to bridges is, at this point, a cliché, but since it's an effective one, let's roll with it. Communication builds this bridge—sharing thoughts and feelings paves the way for connection, but a bridge needs more than structure to become sturdy. Trust and intimacy are the cables, the unseen strength that keeps it stable. Trust lets us know our partner has our back, while intimacy is the closeness, the shared experiences that make the bridge feel welcoming.

These elements all work together: communication builds trust, trust fosters intimacy, and intimacy strengthens the connection, making us want to communicate more openly. It's a cycle that keeps our relationship strong.

## The Role of Trust in Communication

Trust isn't built overnight; it takes time and intentionality. It develops as we consistently experience our partner being reliable, honest, and having our best interests at heart. Knowing they won't intentionally hurt or violate our trust creates a space for vulnerability where we can share our hopes, dreams, and even fears without feeling defensive or guarded. This vulnerability deepens the connection significantly. It allows for intimacy and fosters a sense of "we're in this together." Without trust, a relationship can feel like a house of cards, constantly at risk of collapsing, but with trust as the foundation, our relationship becomes a safe haven, a place where we can truly connect and grow together.

Trust is the glue that holds people that are beneficial for each other together, and here is why:

- **Trust breeds a positive bond:** Knowing your partner has your back fosters forgiveness and a positive outlook. You're more likely to avoid assumptions and overlook minor flaws because you trust their intentions and believe in the strength of your connection.

- **The conflict is calmer:** With trust, disagreements become detours, not dead ends. You're more likely to see things from your partner's perspective and work together on solutions, knowing you're on the same team.

- **Trust unlocks closeness:** Knowing your partner is trustworthy creates a safe haven, and this emotional security allows you to relax and be fully present in the relationship. The shared vulnerability only deepens intimacy and creates a powerful sense of connection. You can truly rely on your partner for comfort, care, and support, knowing they'll be there for you through thick and thin.

When you trust your partner, you don't need to waste precious energy to keep your guard up, but believe in their goodness and intentions. This positive regard allows you to see them in a favorable light and appreciate their unique qualities, which only strengthens the emotional connection and fosters feelings of closeness. Your trust builds them, and theirs builds you.

## Practices for Building and Maintaining Trust

Trust, the cornerstone of healthy relationships, doesn't appear overnight, nor is it something that we can build up and then let it be. It's a continuous investment that is significantly easier (and more pleasurable, if you ask me) to maintain than build from the ground up, but it truly is a two-way street. By consistently demonstrating these qualities, you create a safe space for each other and for trust to blossom in your relationship.

## Open Communication: The Bedrock of Trust

Honesty is the lifeblood of trust, and open communication is the key to achieving it. Sharing openly about your day, thoughts, and feelings allows your partner to feel connected and informed. It is all these seemingly insignificant conversations that fuel the transparency that fosters a sense of security and reduces the need for secrecy. Open communication creates a safe space to discuss not just the ups, but also the downs with all the anxieties or insecurities about the relationship. Working through these concerns together strengthens the bond and builds trust. By openly discussing goals, expectations, and boundaries, you create a sense of "we're in this together" which makes both of you more resilient in the face of anything that might come your way.

## Trust After Mistakes: The Power of Repair

Even the strongest relationships stumble, but when mistakes happen, honesty and owning up to them is key to rebuilding trust. Take ownership by apologizing sincerely and acknowledging your role in the hurt caused because blaming or minimizing the situation erodes trust further. Keep in mind that vague promises ring hollow, so the only way to show genuine remorse is by taking concrete steps to avoid repeating the mistake.

Even the strongest relationships can weather storms that damage trust, but here's how to rebuild connection:

- Be honest and willing to put in the effort together.
- Create new positive memories that strengthen your bond.
- Talk openly, listen attentively, and truly hear each other.
- Find ways to reconnect on an emotional level.
- Keep promises and demonstrate consistent effort.
- Understand yourself better to share authentically.

- Take responsibility for your actions and apologize sincerely.

- Discuss how things will change to prevent repeating mistakes.

Remember, it does take commitment and effort, but if you're willing to break a sweat, you can heal your relationship and emerge stronger than before.

## Enhancing Emotional and Physical Intimacy Through Communication

I'd sometimes love to be able to simplify relationships and compare them to a pizza Margherita where it's pretty easy to see what went into it. However, relationships are more like stews—the best ones can withstand high pressure, and even though they are more or less functional with few ingredients, the more complex the spice mix, the better the outcome. Two such spices are intimacy and communication.

While communication is, in itself, the basic act of sending and receiving messages, in relationships, it's the tool that allows you to build intimacy. This encompasses the entire emotional connection you share with your partner. It's the feeling of closeness, vulnerability, and understanding that develops as you communicate openly and honestly, and can be expressed through emotional support, shared experiences, and even physical affection.

Life must be a seasoned player because it just loves throwing curveballs—work stress, finances, health challenges, negative childhood experiences, traumas, or just feeling swamped. All of these can put a strain on intimacy. While pressing issues need attention, don't let them completely push your relationship aside because even small moments matter. Even though you might not be able to go out of your way and go on a trip, you both always wanted to go on, a quick check-in, sharing a cup of tea, or simply being present with each other can make a big difference. These little connections add up, keeping the flame of intimacy flickering. Remember, nurturing your relationship is an ongoing process, even amid life's challenges.

However, don't despair if your communication or intimacy isn't where you'd like it to be just yet, but rather, explore these steps to get you closer. Because great communication and intimacy are so tightly linked, the steps to achieve one are very similar to achieving the other:

- **Schedule quality time:** Dedicate time each day or week to connect without distractions, where you focus on truly listening and sharing your authentic self.

- **Practice active listening:** Pay attention, avoid interrupting, and reflect back on what you hear to ensure understanding.

- **Express appreciation:** Let your partner know what you value about them, both big and small.

- **Engage in new activities:** Try new hobbies or explore unfamiliar places together, as shared experiences can spark conversation and strengthen bonds.

- **Embrace vulnerability as a relationship superpower:** Share your hopes, dreams, and even your fears, as this openness fosters deeper connection and trust.

- **Patience is part of progress:** Building intimacy and communication takes time and effort. Be patient with yourselves, celebrate small victories, and enjoy the journey of getting closer together.

Every relationship has its peaks and valleys, so don't get discouraged when things don't work out the way they do in Hollywood movies. Keep exploring ways to connect more deeply, even in the small moments, and focus on the positive. Appreciate all the good things you share. Remember, intimacy is a two-way street so it requires both your inputs. Both partners need to put in the effort to create those special moments that strengthen your connection and reward you tenfold through all those shared life experiences.

## Journal Prompt

Research shows that talking openly and sharing your true self with your partner strengthens your connection (Kardan-Souraki et al., 2016). So, on top of encouraging you to invest time in meaningful conversations, asking questions, and really listening to their thoughts and feelings, I'll also provide you with some questions to drop when you feel curious and the time seems right:

- Imagine you have a completely free day to do whatever you enjoy. What activities would fill your day and make it feel truly perfect?

- If you could travel back in time and relive a favorite moment from your childhood, which one would you choose?

- Imagine you stumbled across a crystal ball that could unveil any hidden truth about the future. What burning question would you ask it?

- What are ten bucket list-type experiences that would make your life richer and more fulfilling?

- What's a favorite memory you have from when we were dating?

- If you could unleash your inner artist, what would it be? Painting breathtaking landscapes, writing heart-wrenching stories, or something totally different?

# Chapter 10:
# Setting Boundaries and Respecting Limits

The word *boundaries* might conjure up images of cold, isolating walls. While they do create a separation between you and others, that separation is there for a reason. Healthy boundaries are more like fences—they establish clear lines that protect your emotional and physical space. Just like a well-maintained fence allows a garden to flourish, boundaries allow relationships to thrive. They ensure you have the time and energy to nurture your own needs and interests, which in turn fosters a healthier, happier you to share with the world.

## The Importance of Boundaries in Relationships

Boundaries exist in all relationships, but they're especially important with romantic partners. They're clear lines we communicate to show what's okay and what's not, for both us and our partner. These unspoken rules keep us feeling like "us" and foster respect, safety, and clear expectations. Our relationship is like a team with three members: us, our partner, and the bond we share. Boundaries define a healthy space for each member, allowing the team to truly thrive.

There are numerous benefits to setting boundaries, but all in all, these are the main changes you'll notice once you set healthy ones:

- You become more independent and less reliant on others, which can improve your self-esteem and make your relationships stronger.

- They help to communicate your expectations to others and this can mean avoiding misunderstandings and conflict.

- They can help you to feel more in control of your life and more confident in yourself.

- They can help you to protect yourself from physical and emotional harm.

- They can help to make it clear who is responsible for what in a relationship, which will also protect both of you from resentment and conflict.

- They can elicit self–awareness and help you be more in tune with your own wants, needs, thoughts, and feelings, and this often means making better decisions for yourself.

Setting boundaries is crucial for both of you, but not all boundaries are healthy. If a boundary is limiting and trying to control your partner's actions or choices, like dictating how they spend time, dress, or even act, that's not a healthy boundary. If your partner dictates your boundaries, that's another red flag for communication issues. Healthy boundaries don't seek to control or restrict a person's freedom.

## Healthy Types of Boundaries

Healthy boundaries are communicated clearly, with respect for each other's needs, so they should be or feel like they're chipping away at one's independence.

## Physical Boundaries

These boundaries are all about feeling safe and comfortable. Physical boundaries could be something as simple as preferring handshakes over hugs, or letting your partner know you need a break during a hike. Physical space matters too! Maybe you have a designated "me-time" zone in your bedroom, or you'd prefer your partner not to leave their stuff in your workspace. Just like with friends, clear communication about your physical needs strengthens your connection and keeps the romance happy.

## Sexual Boundaries

In a romantic relationship, intimacy goes beyond the physical. Sexual boundaries are all about open communication and mutual respect. This includes always getting consent before getting physical, and checking in with your partner to ensure they're comfortable throughout. Even long-term couples should keep the conversation going. Talk about your preferences for intimacy, how often you'd like to be physical, and your preferred methods of contraception. Boundaries in the bedroom can keep the spark alive by ensuring everyone feels safe, respected, and heard.

## Emotional Boundaries

Boundaries are also there to protect you from emotional overload. Let's say you politely decline a second date; you don't need to take responsibility for their reaction. It's okay to say, "I understand you're disappointed, but my decision is firm." Healthy boundaries in love keep you feeling safe, respected, and emotionally balanced.

In a loving relationship, emotional boundaries aren't walls; they're guideposts for healthy connection. They ensure your partner respects your feelings and comfort zone. If you work from home, focusing is a challenge to begin with, so an emotional boundary might sound like, "Honey, I can't talk about this now, I need to concentrate. Can we discuss it later?"

## Financial Boundaries

Love is grand, but finances and possessions need clear lines too. Material boundaries are about respecting each other's stuff, like money, clothes, or your car. Maybe you're super generous naturally, but constantly lending things can lead to resentment. Setting boundaries can sound like, "Sure, borrow my charger, but please return it" or a gentle "Hey, I can't swing a loan for new shoes right now." Healthy boundaries in love mean respecting what belongs to each other, keeping the financial stress low, and the trust high.

## Time Boundaries

Date nights are awesome, but you both need "me-time" too. Time boundaries help you prioritize work, self-care, and your relationship. Imagine a crazy week at work—a healthy time boundary might be saying, "Love the party invite, but I need a recharge weekend.

Raincheck?" Boundaries can also be about setting limits within dates. Maybe you need to focus before a big presentation and ask your partner, "Can we discuss this important thing after dinner?" Healthy time boundaries in love ensure you both feel supported and have space to recharge, keeping the spark alive.

Boundaries are more like living things than statues. As your relationship grows and life throws curveballs, you might need to adjust them, and this is especially true in long-term partnerships. The key to it all is open communication. Talk to your partner about any changes you want to make, explaining the reason behind it. This keeps them informed and helps you navigate boundaries together, strengthening your connection.

## Communicating Boundaries Effectively

When you invest time and energy into getting to know yourself better, you can create boundaries that ensure your needs are met and your love blossoms. But first, ask yourself: What makes me tick? What qualities do I admire in others? What kind of treatment do I deserve? (For example, if you value independence, you might want clear financial boundaries with your partner). What are your dealbreakers? What makes you feel fulfilled? Understanding your values helps you set boundaries that protect your well-being. (For example, if you need quiet time to recharge, you might set time boundaries with a partner who needs constant company.)

Introducing boundaries early in a relationship is ideal, before habits form and emotions run deep, but late is still better than never. Boundaries, even introduced later, can strengthen your connection by preventing resentment. It's all about clear communication and respect for each other's needs. Rushed explanations or vague requests are not ideal for making your needs understood. Talk openly with your partner about what you need, as this helps them respect your boundaries and keeps the love unencumbered.

## Choose Your Timing Wisely

Timing is everything, especially with boundaries. Trying to discuss boundaries in the heat of an argument is certainly not the best recipe for understanding. It's better to wait until you're both calm and collected, as this allows for a focused conversation where you can clearly explain your needs and hear your partner's perspective.

## Do Your Homework

Boundary talks can feel daunting, so if nerves are getting the best of you, come prepared. Jot down your key points beforehand, as this helps organize your thoughts and ensures you clearly communicate what boundaries you need. Think of it as a gentle roadmap for the conversation, ensuring your needs are clear, heard, and understood.

## Delivery Supports Content

When discussing boundaries, focus on "I" statements, not accusatory "you" statements. Instead of saying, "You never help with chores!" try, "I feel overwhelmed when I have to handle all the housework alone." As mentioned previously, "I" statements highlight your feelings and needs, making it easier for your partner to understand your perspective.

## Crystal Clear Communication

Vague boundaries create confusion. Instead of a mumbling, "I need more space," be crystal clear. Try, "I feel uncomfortable when I work (or any other activity) and you enter my office/room unannounced. Could you please knock first? It would give me some privacy and respect for my space." This calmly explains the behavior you need to change and sets a clear expectation. A firm but kind tone shows you're serious without coming across as accusatory.

Boundaries, as with many things in relationships, are a two-way street, so when you set a boundary, it's only natural that your partner might have questions. Remember, you don't owe them justifications, but explaining your feelings can bridge understanding. For example, "This boundary is important to me because..." Be open to each other's opinions, and instead of assuming your partner's feelings, simply ask. "Does this request seem unreasonable? Does it clash with something you need?" Healthy relationships are about mutual respect, the drive to understand each other, and a space where both your needs can be met.

## Respecting Your Partner's Boundaries

As a rule of thumb, when healthy boundaries are set, both partners ask permission and express themselves honestly. They also consider each other's feelings, and celebrate each other's wins with gratitude, and give each other space to be themselves, respecting differences in opinion and perspective. They also hold each other accountable for actions and work through emotions together.

We sometimes fall into the trap of thinking that our partner has it all figured out, so they don't have a reason to have a bad day. But they do have a reason and they do have a bad day here and there. Not only that, but it's more likely that their lives are as "figured out" as ours are, so we both deserve the same understanding, patience, and ability to set and have our boundaries respected.

### Lead Conversations Through the Lens of Curiosity

Embrace curiosity in all aspects of life! Instead of assuming what's okay with your partner, ask open-ended questions. A simple "Is this alright with you?" will do wonders. When you respect someone's boundaries, it shows you value their comfort, fostering a more open and trusting relationship. This is an ongoing conversation, where you both learn and adapt, and the more you ask, the better you understand their limits. Remember, clear communication is key to navigating boundaries.

### Nonverbal Discomfort Displays

Not everyone feels comfortable verbally asserting their boundaries, but that doesn't mean they don't have any. Pay close attention to nonverbal cues: Is their posture closed off with their shoulders pushed forward and hands crossed in front of their body? Are they avoiding eye contact? Do they have a furrowed brow? Notice fidgeting or nervous laughter as these subtle gestures can signal someone feeling uneasy. Sometimes, even a sudden lack of conversation or engagement can indicate a pushed boundary. By becoming more aware of non-verbal communication, you can pick up on discomfort before it escalates. This allows you to adjust your behavior and respect their boundaries, even if they haven't explicitly stated them.

## Bring Empathy Into It All

Not everyone experiences emotions in the same way, and boundaries can seem random at times, but here's the secret: a little empathy goes a long way. Think back to a time you felt uncomfortable or disrespected; maybe someone crossed a personal line. Imagine that feeling, even if the situation is different. By putting yourself in your partner's shoes, you can cultivate empathy and respond with kindness. This understanding fosters a safe space where boundaries are respected, even if not always explicitly explained.

## Apologize and Forgive Yourself for Mistakes

Neither of us is perfect and behaving as we should all the time, so when you unknowingly or mistakenly cross a boundary, a sincere apology goes a long way. Acknowledge you crossed a line and express that you'll try harder next time, as this shows respect and rebuilds trust quickly. Remember not to beat yourself up, either. Your intention was never to hurt your partner, and even the best at boundaries make mistakes. Instead, use this experience as a learning opportunity because the more chances to learn about each other you have, the more chances you have to propel your relationship into a healthy one.

Respecting boundaries isn't a chore or a limit; it's a love language. Therapist Cristen Smith puts it perfectly: "Respecting someone's boundaries, even if they seem strange, shows them they matter" (Marie, 2022). By listening and honoring their limits, you communicate that their well-being and comfort are important to you. This builds invaluable trust, strengthens your connection, and makes it sustainable in the long run, all while fostering a healthy, loving relationship.

## Journal Prompt

Let's ponder on a few questions that will help us become aware of our boundaries, which is really, the first step in setting them:

- Saying no can be tough. What situations make it especially difficult for you?

- Do you find it hard to apologize and forgive yourself for mistakes?

- Do you have a personal motto that guides your actions? What is a recent example of how you've put it into practice?

# Chapter 11:
# Communicating Love and Appreciation

"I love you" is a timeless classic, but don't underestimate the magic of specifics. When you have the chance, tell your partner what you admire about them—their kindness, humor, or intelligence. Express gratitude for their efforts, big or small. A simple "Thank you for making dinner" or "I appreciate you always listening" goes a long way. Words are powerful, but actions solidify them. Life inevitably gets busy, but don't forget to carve out dedicated time to simply connect. Put away distractions and focus on each other, enjoy a shared activity, have a deep conversation, or cuddle on the couch.

## Expressing Love and Appreciation in Everyday Interactions

Making appreciation a daily habit strengthens the love you share. Even better, research by Emmons & Stern suggests a powerful feedback loop, so the more we express gratitude, the more we recognize the positive in our partner and the relationship. This, in turn, increases our overall well-being and resilience, making us even more likely to feel and express gratitude (2013).

To truly strengthen relationships, we need to express our love and appreciation in ways that are meaningful for us and our partner. The key is finding the right fit for the situation. Taking your partner to their favorite restaurant is a fantastic way to show appreciation for their support, but if you both feel more in your element at a picnic with a view, the second is the more meaningful option. Think of expressing gratitude like different social tools. A simple "thank you" is a handy wrench, useful for everyday situations. But sometimes, you need a specialized tool, like a heartfelt letter or a thoughtful gift, to show your appreciation in a way that truly resonates with your partner and strengthens your connection.

## Unexpected Acts of Kindness

Spreading kindness is good for us too, as studies by Rowland & Curry show, random acts of kindness boost happiness (2019). Helping a stranger with groceries, donating clothes, or simply offering directions—these small gestures add up to a big boost in well-being for both you and the recipient. When the recipient is your loved one, the reward is tenfold for both of you. So next time you see a chance to be kind, seize it!

## Lead Life With Respect for Everyone

Just because we've become comfortable to be our unguarded selves with our partner, it doesn't mean treating them with any less respect than a stranger. Small gestures like listening attentively, offering help with chores, or simply putting away our phones during dinner show that we value their time and well-being. These everyday courtesies strengthen our connection and create a space where respect and love can flourish, and appreciation is written in capital letters.

Say "thank you" as many times as you feel thankful for something your partner did, or simply for them, and when "thank you" feels like yesterday's news, replace it with:

- This truly means a lot to me.

- I'm so incredibly grateful for what you've done.

- Feeling your support gives me so much strength. You're truly amazing.

- I'm deeply touched that you thought of me.

- You're amazing, and I'm so lucky to have you in my life.

- It's amazing how well you get me.

It might seem cheesy at first if you were not used to such love and appreciation displays in your family growing up, but saying "thank you" and showing appreciation isn't just polite; it boosts our well-being, our mind, body, and social connections. Psychologically, gratitude reduces stress and increases happiness. Socially, expressing appreciation strengthens relationships, and physically, it can even lead to better sleep and a stronger immune system (Wood et al., 2010). Next time you feel grateful, don't hold back, but express it with with confidence. You're doing yourself, your partner, and the world a favor.

## Understanding and Speaking Your Partner's Love Language

Love languages have long been decoded, and it all started when counselor Gary Chapman noticed that the couples he was seeing were more or less following five patterns. Do compliments make your partner blossom? Or maybe they crave quality time or helpful gestures? The key is understanding what makes them tick and express love in a "language" in which they truly understand how much you appreciate them.

### Words of Affirmation

This love language is all about expressing affection verbally. Does your partner light up at compliments or appreciate a heartfelt note? This love language thrives on praise, encouragement, and kind words, so make their day with compliments, highlight their strengths, or leave them a sweet love note. Words of affirmation are simple ways to show you care, even if poetry isn't your forte, and to make them feel cherished.

### Quality Time

If you, too, crave connection and not just company, you might speak the "quality time" language. People with this love language value focused attention. It's not about hours spent together, but truly being present. Ditch the phone, tune in, and listen with your heart, not just your ears. Plan special dates, engage in shared activities, or simply have a conversation where they feel your undivided attention. Remember, quality time is about connecting on a deeper level, getting into those deep and meaningful conversations, and showing you cherish their company.

## Physical Touch

If you need a hug to say "I love you," physical touch might be your love language. People who speak this language crave affection—cuddles, handholding, massages, or simply a reassuring touch. Forget fancy dates; a movie night snuggled on the couch might be their ideal way to connect. Physical touch is a way to show you care and feel connected, so next time you see your partner, reach out for a hand and let them know you're there for them and you care.

## Acts of Service

Do you speak the language of helpfulness? "Acts of service" is about showing love through actions. Does your partner feel loved when you take out the trash or make them coffee? People with this language appreciate gestures that lighten their load. Helping with chores, running errands, or simply doing something thoughtful shows you care and makes their life easier. They likely express love through acts of service for others too, so return the favor and show them you appreciate their kind heart.

## Receiving Gifts

Gifts can speak volumes for some, and it is through thoughtful presents that they feel most loved. It's not about materialism; it's the effort behind the gift. A small, well-chosen token shows you pay attention and care. They likely put thought into gifts for others too, so when you can, reciprocate. Picking out something special tells them you know them and cherish the connection, and these even inexpensive gifts become treasured memories, a reminder of your love and thoughtfulness.

These five love languages offer different fuels for different people. By understanding what makes *you* feel loved (words of affirmation, quality time, etc.), you unlock the key to a happier relationship. When you're clear about your needs, you can communicate them to your partner. "I feel most appreciated when you compliment my effort" or "Spending quality time with you, just the two of us, makes me feel cherished" are clear ways to express your desires. This self-awareness empowers you to guide your partner in expressing love in a way that truly fills their tank too. The result is a stronger connection, deeper appreciation, and a relationship fueled by love in its most fulfilling form for you, without strong sentiments ever getting lost in translation.

## The Impact of Gratitude on Relationship Satisfaction

Feeling grateful and expressing our gratitude already feel great to begin with, but when we're sure our gratitude reaches its source, is an even better feeling. According to a University of Illinois study, feeling appreciated by your partner strengthens your relationship's immune system. People who feel valued are more resilient to stress, both in the moment and over time, and this appreciation shield protects your connection from everyday bumps and long-term challenges (2022).

There are a number of studies that, essentially, encourage us to count our blessings and impart this feeling of gratitude as much as possible. A grateful mindset acts like a shield against negativity, so it's maybe no surprise that a 2010 review linked gratitude with less depression, anxiety, and even substance abuse. It can even help us cope with trauma (Wood et al., 2010). More recent research backs this up, showing a strong connection between a grateful outlook and overall emotional and social well-being for both partners. If this weren't enough, people with good relationships tend to live longer (Algoe, 2012). So next time you feel down, take a moment to appreciate the good things in your life—it might be just the boost you both needed.

Let's look at the Gottman Institute again and see what they have to say about gratitude. Do you remember when I mentioned that one of the more significant signs of an imminent divorce was contempt? Well, showing gratitude in relationships protects you against just that. The Gottman method encourages you to cultivate positive thoughts about your partner that often translate to showing appreciation, that in turn is strengthening your bond and preventing negativity from creeping in (Gottman & Gottman, 2015).

It seems like gratitude transcends cultural norms or customs, and I couldn't be more glad for it. While a plethora of studies from around the world reached the same conclusions, a Hong Kong study found a key to happy relationships: saying "thank you"! While simply feeling grateful for your partner helps, researchers discovered that actually expressing that gratitude boosts satisfaction even more, but the secret is in it being authentic (Leong et al., 2019).

When we voice appreciation for our loved ones, it strengthens the bond and makes everyone feel happier. It's the best kind of win–win! We should aim to openly and often share our gratitude with those closest to us, but also spread the love to friends, family, and even colleagues.

## Journal Prompt

Let's actively spark joy in your love life today. Take a few minutes to appreciate your partner. What makes them special? Write down a list of things you're grateful for—their humor, support, or simply being them. Sharing this list is a sweet way to show you care and strengthen your connection.

# Step 5:
# Practical Applications

# Chapter 12:
# Communication in Different Relationship Stages

As you get to know each other better and as your daily habits mold and adapt to each other, communication transforms as well. The more quality time and talks you have, the easier communication becomes. The more energy you invest in understanding each other, the more you speak the same language.

## Early Relationship Communication

First impressions are more than just what we see. Early interactions on dates or online are filled with hidden messages, even if we don't realize it. We subtly communicate our hopes, fears, and desires for the relationship, both verbally and nonverbally. It's natural to put our best foot forward, but pretending to be someone we're not can't last.

Dating can be vulnerable, but honesty is key. While we might try to hide insecurities, our true selves eventually shine through, both in what we say and how we say it. This is why paying close attention to all communication, both words and body language, is crucial in getting to know our potential partners. These subtle cues can reveal a lot about what someone is really looking for and feeling, helping us build a stronger connection based on authenticity.

**Initial Red Flags**

Do you feel like you're being swept off your feet too soon? Slow down for a moment. Hearing "I've never met anyone like you" on a date might feel flattering, but it can also be a red flag. Is this person genuinely interested in you or just filling a void? Are they idealizing you instead of seeing the real you? Being put on a pedestal so quickly can be a sign of unhealthy neediness or even narcissism. Take a breath and ask yourself: Is this a real connection, or just a fantasy? Healthy relationships take time to build, so trust your gut if things seem too intense too fast.

We often have a sense about someone, even if we try to ignore it. That initial gut feeling—a thought, a reaction—is usually pretty accurate. It tells us what we want, what we fear, or how we truly feel about the connection, but sometimes, we push those feelings aside, hoping communication will fix things. The same goes for nonverbal cues. Micro-expressions, those tiny facial reactions that last fractions of a second, can reveal our true emotions even if we try to hide them. Ignoring these red flags, both internal and external, can lead to problems down the line.

Conflict, disappointment, or a lack of passion in the relationship might be signs that we weren't honest with ourselves or each other from the start. Eventually, when the honeymoon phase comes to an end, the truth comes out—sometimes quietly, sometimes with a bang. Hurtful words might fly, but the relief of acknowledging incompatibility can be bittersweet. Building a strong relationship takes open communication and self-awareness, so ignoring our intuition, in the beginning, will only lead to a painful ending later.

**Expressing Emotional Needs**

While sexual experiences can be a draw early on, relying solely on physical intimacy can backfire. Sex is a form of communication, but deeper or emotional needs often get left unspoken. Using sex to avoid emotional connection might feel good in the moment, but it's not sustainable because long-term relationships need more than just physical compatibility.

Don't be afraid to express your emotional needs and build a deeper connection for a truly fulfilling relationship, but I appreciate that honest communication from the start is tricky. It's hard to define exactly what you both need and want in a relationship, let alone say it out loud. But being truthful, even when it's difficult, allows your partner to truly hear you and vice versa. Can they accept your needs? Can you accept theirs? This open communication fosters respect and allows you both to truly assess for compatibility, creating fertile ground for a strong, lasting connection.

# Communicating During Major Life Changes

The social script tells us life follows a predictable path: college, love, marriage, house, kids, retirement, etc. but life, much like the weather, can be unpredictable. We might not meet our soulmates in our 20s, 30s, or even 40s, face challenges like infertility, or get thrown curveballs like job relocations or unexpected losses. Life is a messy, beautiful mix of joy, stability, and unexpected twists. We crave security, but detours and setbacks are simply inevitable. To navigate these transitions, a strong support system is crucial and often, we turn to our partners as we build our families.

However, when both partners are facing challenges, it can be hard to connect and offer each other the support we both need. Just as we prepare for different weather patterns, we can prepare for life's uncertainties. Building a strong support network beyond just our partner and include our friends, family, or therapist, can provide a safety net during emotional storms. Of course, open communication with our partner is also key—by acknowledging shared frustrations and working together, we can weather any season life throws our way.

## Invest in Communication Quality Before Transitions

Before a big move or unexpected event, take time to understand each other's worries. "What would make this easier for you?" is a great conversation starter. Even if there's no warning, find a quiet moment to check in with each other. Can you create a support system for each other? Don't forget the kids, if they're in the picture. Give everyone a voice to express their needs and find solutions together.

## Individual and Couple Quality Time

Even amid chaos, steal 15 minutes to connect. Cuddle, chat, or eat together without any distraction, so needless to say, make this time phone-free. However, don't forget yourself either. Take time alone to recharge, sleep, eat well, exercise, and do everything that you can to keep your mind sharp and adaptable. Read, learn something new, and stay energized to tackle anything life throws your way.

## Plan but Be Open for Adjustments

Is your child heading off to college? Don't just see it as an empty nest, but use this lead time to talk about the future together. How can you rekindle those passions you've put aside because you prioritized other aspects of your lives? Imagine all the possibilities: more travel, hobbies, or simply reconnecting as a couple. Discuss the practicalities, too: smaller grocery runs, redecorating the spare room, or planning long-awaited adventures. Remember, life rarely goes exactly as planned, so be flexible and adjust together. This transition can be a chance to strengthen your bond and create a new chapter in your relationship.

## Ask For Outside Support if Needed

Do you feel stuck trying to navigate a big change? You don't have to do it alone! Support groups and therapy can be lifesavers during stressful transitions. Whether it's facing an empty nest or a job loss, these resources offer guidance and connection with others going through similar challenges. You'll gain valuable coping skills, learn from other people's experiences, strengthen your bond as a couple, and emerge feeling empowered to tackle the future together.

## Enjoy Change as Opportunity

Not all changes are created equal; some transitions, like welcoming a child, are filled with joy (and maybe a little sleep deprivation), so don't forget to take a moment to appreciate this new adventure together—that tiny miracle in your arms is a reminder of the amazing things life has to offer. Even stressful changes, like a big move, can be reframed as opportunities. See it as a chance to explore a new place, meet new people, and rediscover yourselves as a couple. Embrace the adventure, the challenges, and the growth that comes with navigating life's twists and turns together.

By focusing on the positive and supporting each other, you can turn any transition into a chance to strengthen your bond and create lasting memories.

## Long-Term Relationship Communication

Long-term love is beautiful, but sometimes the chats can feel a bit "been there, done that." How can you reignite the conversation spark and rediscover the joy of talking to your partner? You can turn everyday talk into heartfelt exchanges. Communication is paramount in relationships, but it's about more than just avoiding silence. Look for opportunities in daily routines to connect on a deeper level. This could be a dedicated chat time without distractions, or simply asking open-ended questions about their day. Delve into each other's thoughts, feelings, and dreams. What are you passionate about lately? What challenges are you facing? Discussing these deeper things fosters a sense of intimacy and understanding.

### Be Genuinely Interested in Your Partner's Day

Ditch the "How was your day?" routine and ask follow-up questions to explore their day's ups, downs, and funny moments. This shows genuine interest and helps you understand their world. Every detail, from work challenges to little victories, becomes a chance to connect and strengthen your bond.

### Create New Routines

When you're feeling stuck in a conversation rut, it's time to break free from the routine and try something new together. Taking a cooking class, going for a hike, or visiting a museum can spark a wellspring of conversation. You'll share challenges, triumphs, and maybe some laughs along the way. These new experiences not only create memories but also give you plenty to talk about, fostering connection and strengthening your bond as you navigate unfamiliar territory together.

## Draw Excitement From Making Plans

Light a fire under your conversations by talking about future dreams together. Is there a trip you've always wanted to take? Brainstorm your perfect home or dream job because discussing these things reveals hidden desires and goals. Sharing your hopes and ambitions creates a sense of connection and sparks exciting conversations about the future you'll build together. It's not just about the destination; it's about aligning your dreams and understanding each other's deepest desires.

## Discuss Everything That's on Your Minds

Whenever you're feeling chatty, talk about what's happening in the world together. From new movies to political debates, current events offer endless conversation starters. Sharing your thoughts and opinions can create lively discussions, strengthening your intellectual connection. Don't force it though; if you have other interests, rather go ahead and explore those. The key is finding a balance between current events and keeping the conversation flowing naturally. This can help you understand each other's perspectives and stay engaged with the world around you.

## Same Old but Still New Active Listening

If you want to turn small talk into something special, practice active listening. Don't wait for your turn to speak, but truly focus on what your partner is saying. Try to understand their feelings and emotions, and respond thoughtfully. Show them you're engaged by remembering key points. This shows you care and want to understand their world. In return, they'll feel heard and appreciated, creating a safe space for deeper conversations.

By making conversation a priority and putting in the effort, you can keep the spark alive and build an even stronger connection with your long-term love. Remember, a successful relationship isn't just about knowing everything—it's about continually learning and growing together, one conversation at a time.

## Journal Prompt

You and your partner are curled up on the couch, laughing hysterically over a scene in that new movie you both wanted to see. Or maybe you're reminiscing about that epic road trip you took together, the one with the flat tire and the breathtaking sunset. These shared moments, big and small, are the glue that strengthens your bond.

Let's explore some prompts that spark the same conversations that bring these experiences to life. They'll help you rediscover the joy of connecting with your loved one through shared laughter, adventures, and even challenges:

- Can you think of a time when you felt closer to your partner? What were you doing together?

- What are some things you're curious about that you could explore with your partner?

- How can having things in common make your relationship more fulfilling?

Chapter 13:
# Exercises and Practice

Every couple hits bumps in the road, and that's absolutely normal! But constant fights or feeling unheard can chip away at the happiness you share and these struggles often stem from communication issues. Left unchecked, they can lead to anxiety and distance, so, before this becomes our reality, let's dive into some exercises that make your relationship and both of you more resilient.

While this theory comes from the finance world, it resonated with me so much that even now, many years later, I remember reading about it and my enthusiasm as if it was yesterday. Stephen Covey, a renowned businessman and author, encourages us to imagine our relationship with someone as a bank account. The Emotional Bank Account theory suggests that every interaction makes a deposit or withdrawal. Positive actions like kindness, honesty, and support act like deposits, building trust and strengthening the connection. Conversely, negativity like criticism, anger, or ignoring our partner's needs makes withdrawals. Over time, too many withdrawals can lead to emotional bankruptcy, causing disconnection and resentment (2004).

The key is to make more (and more qualitative) deposits than withdrawals. By showing appreciation, actively listening, and keeping commitments, we create a secure emotional foundation for a thriving relationship.

## Practical Exercises for Improving Communication Skills

Does communication need any more cheerleading when it comes to being the secret to lasting and meaningful relationships?

## Affirmations of Fondness

Of all the communication pitfalls couples face, contempt is the worst. It's a subtle but potent poison that can erode respect and love. Even a sarcastic comment or an eye roll can be a sign of contempt, used to belittle a partner and feel superior, but there's a clear antidote to contempt: appreciation! These are simple phrases that highlight what you admire about your partner. Instead of a generic "I love you," be more specific and say, "I love it when you..."

## The Eye Connection Challenge

Ready to explore a deeper connection with your partner? This powerful exercise, known as the Eye Connection Challenge, can help you reconnect on a nonverbal level. You'll need two chairs facing each other, a quiet, distraction-free space, and a timer set for five minutes.

Sit down in the chairs facing each other. Close your eyes briefly, take a deep breath together, and then open your eyes to meet your partner's gaze. For the next 5 minutes, focus solely on eye contact. Don't talk, just observe and feel. Notice the details of their eyes, the emotions they convey. Are there any changes in their expression? Does eye contact evoke any emotions? A sense of calm, a spark of connection?

When the timer goes off, gently break eye contact, and take turns sharing what you experienced during the silent gaze. Describe what you saw in their eyes, any emotions you felt, or even if you felt nothing at all. When your partner shares, give them your full attention. Listen without judgment and with an open heart.

## Mirroring Exercise

Are you feeling stuck in a communication rut with your partner? Mirroring, a technique where you take turns really listening to each other, works wonders in ensuring you understand each other. Here's how it works:

- **One person speaks:** They express their feelings and explain their perspective fully.

- **Active listening:** The other person starts by summarizing what they heard with a phrase like "So, what I hear you saying is..."

- **Clarification:** If everything seems clear, the listener asks, "Tell me more" to encourage further explanation.

- **Back-and-forth continues:** This process repeats until the speaker feels fully heard.

Why does it work? Mirroring helps the brain relax because it feels like what's being said is actually being understood. This can be a powerful tool for couples to rebuild trust, empathy, and a stronger connection.

## Role–Playing Scenarios for Conflict Resolution

There's more to communication than meets the eye, and how we use our words can ensure a smooth sail or a bumpy road. These role-playing exercises let you practice resolving conflict in a safe space. Choose one of the situations that might cause a disagreement. Take turns playing both Partner A and Partner B in the scenario and use the template "I feel [emotion] when you [partner's action]." Really hear each other out and try mirroring what you hear to confirm understanding. Then, focus on finding a solution that works for both of you. If you need to think before responding, that's okay. At the end of the day, the goal is teamwork, not winning. This kind of exercise can help you develop better routines for working through disagreements in the future:

- Partner A promised to call Partner B at a specific time, but they never did. Partner B tried to reach them but couldn't get a hold of them.

- Partner A frequently talks down to Partner B, explains things in a way that implies Partner B doesn't understand, or rolls their eyes at their questions.

- Partner A constantly needs to know where Partner B is and what they're doing, and gets upset if Partner B has plans that don't include them.

- Partner A struggles to express affection in a way that feels meaningful to Partner B. They might not say "I love you" often enough, or avoid physical touch.

- Partner A seems oblivious to how their actions impact Partner B. They might leave dirty dishes piled up or walk through the door without taking off their shoes, despite knowing it creates extra work for Partner B.

- Partner A expresses a lot of anxiety about their looks, constantly checking the mirror, seeking reassurance about their appearance, or being overly critical of themselves. This can be draining for Partner B and make them feel like their happiness is dependent on external validation.

**There's No Rug to Sweep Things Under**

Unresolved conflict can fester and lead to bigger blowups down the line. Address problems head-on and ideally, discuss and resolve issues soon after they arise. If that's not possible, agree on a specific time to talk it out later.

**Remember When? Rekindle the Spark**

Life gets busy, and sometimes the flame of what first drew you together can dim. Arguments and disagreements can take center stage, pushing those cherished feelings aside. Reminding yourselves of why you fell in love can be a game-changer, and Dr. Gottman suggests these questions to help couples reconnect (Gottman & Gottman, 2015):

- What sparked your love story? Think back to those first exciting moments. What made you click?

- Early days magic: Reflect on your early years together. What were some special memories?

- What made a difference then? Consider how you interacted in the past that felt positive and supportive.

- What's good now? Take stock of the present. What are some things you appreciate about each other now?

- Showing you care: How do you express your love currently?

- Feeling loved: What actions make you feel cherished by your partner?

- Love languages in action: Discuss ways to show affection that resonate with each other.

Strong connections are life's safety net; they provide unwavering support, a listening ear in dark times, and a loud cheer in victories. These relationships allow you to see each other, flaws and all, fostering growth through shared experiences. A long-term partner pushes you to be your best self, while a deep emotional connection offers comfort and stability. In a world that can feel isolating, these bonds are a powerful reminder: you're not alone!

## Journaling Prompts: Positive Self–Talk and Growth

Your inner voice shapes your outer world, and the way you speak to yourself sets the tone for your day. Positive self-talk boosts your confidence and shapes how you interact with the world, so, let's fill our heads with encouragement so strong that it reflects in everything we do.

This constant inner chatter, from task instructions to random observations, is your self-talk. It's the voice you hear most, but rarely consider, so write down the next affirmations in your journal and read them every time you need a check–in with yourself:

- My mind is open to new possibilities. (Empowers the idea of change.)

- Stepping outside my comfort zone was scary, but I'm glad I did. (Highlights courage and initiative.)

- This may not have been the plan, but I gained valuable insights. (Focuses on the learning experience.)

- There's still progress to be made, and I'm celebrating the steps I've taken. (Acknowledges growth and self-appreciation.)

- I am capable, and I have the strength to overcome this. (Emphasizes resilience and self-belief.)

- A new day brings a fresh start, armed with yesterday's lessons. (Focuses on using past experiences for future success.)

- All I can do is give it my best shot. (Highlights effort and commitment.)

- Their reactions are out of my control, but I can control my own path. (Focuses on personal agency.)

- This is an exciting chance to explore something uncharted! (Highlights the positive side of change.)

- Challenges offer opportunities to learn and evolve. (Focuses on personal growth and development.)

# Conclusion: The Journey of Continuous Improvement

Mastering communication in a romantic relationship isn't just an exotic destination; it's also a lifelong and diverse journey. There will be miscommunications, misunderstandings, and moments of frustration along the way, but with the right tools, dedication, and effort, you can transform these challenges into opportunities for deeper connection. It's about continuous growth, understanding, and always being curious about each other.

Communication isn't merely a tool for sharing information, but a dynamic process that shapes connection, intimacy, and growth. Throughout this exploration, we have delved into the intricacies of verbal and nonverbal communication, the significance of active listening, and the power of empathy. We've discussed the importance of setting boundaries, expressing gratitude, and resolving conflict constructively. These are not merely tools but essential components of a thriving relationship. Yet, this journey is far from over.

Communication is a living entity, evolving with the complexities of our lives, so it's only natural that it requires constant nurturing and adaptation. Just as we grow and change, so too should our communication styles. What works today might not be as effective tomorrow, especially as we continue decoding our attachment styles as well. Regardless of where you are in this journey right now, celebrate your successes, learn from your challenges, and approach each interaction with a spirit of curiosity, openness, and a willingness to learn.

Remember, perfection isn't something we should strive for, and the healthiest thing we can do is place it in a box labeled "unattainable," but progress is always possible. Even when it doesn't feel like much progress is being made, the simple act of trying is progress. Every conversation, every time you actively listen to your partner, and every shared experience, is an opportunity to deepen your connection. It's all about creating a safe space where both of you are comfortable to open up, and feel heard, valued, and understood. This is how you build a foundation of trust and respect that can weather any storm. However, let's not forget that healthy communication is also about finding joy in the shared journey of discovery.

Ultimately, effective communication is the cornerstone of a fulfilling and enduring partnership. It's about building a shared language of love, respect, and understanding. By embracing the journey of improvement, you're investing in the health and happiness of your relationship, and this is the kind of investment that yields immeasurable returns in the form of deeper intimacy, shared experiences, and a love that grows stronger with time.

So, continue to explore, to learn, to grow, and to communicate authentically. The most beautiful relationships are those where two people are constantly evolving and growing together and your relationship deserves nothing less. This relationship is a masterpiece in progress, and with each brushstroke of communication, you create a more beautiful and enduring work of art.

For more resources that may be useful on your journey, please visit www.modernflowcollective.com/freetools.

# References

Algoe, S. B. (2012). Find, remind, and bind: The functions of gratitude in everyday relationships. *Social and Personality Psychology Compass, 6*(6), 455–469. https://doi.org/10.1111/j.1751-9004.2012.00439.x

*APA dictionary of psychology.* (n.d.). American Psychological Association. https://dictionary.apa.org/nonverbal-communication

Aristotle. (2012). *Aristotle's Nicomachean Ethics.* University of Chicago Press.

Barton, A. W., Jenkins, A. I. C., Gong, Q., Sutton, N. C., & Beach, S. R. (2023). The protective effects of perceived gratitude and expressed gratitude for relationship quality among African American couples. *Journal of Social and Personal Relationships, 40*(5), 1622–1644. https://doi.org/10.1177/02654075221131288

Bowlby, J. (1982). Attachment and loss: Retrospect and prospect. *American Journal of Orthopsychiatry, 52*(4), 664–678. https://doi.org/10.1111/j.1939-0025.1982.tb01456.x

Brown, B. (2021). *Atlas of the heart: Mapping meaningful connection and the language of human experience.* Random House.

Caughlin, J. P., Mikucki-Enyart, S. L., & Vangelisti, A. L. (2013, Second Edition). *The SAGE handbook of conflict communication: Integrating theory, research, and practice.* SAGE Publications, Inc.

Cherry, K. (2023a, February 22). *Types of nonverbal communication.* Verywell Mind. https://www.verywellmind.com/types-of-nonverbal-communication-2795397

Cherry, K. (2023b, February 22). *What is attachment theory?* Verywell Mind. https://www.verywellmind.com/what-is-attachment-theory-2795337

Cherry, K. (2023c, June 29). *Emotions and types of emotional responses.* Verywell Mind. https://www.verywellmind.com/what-are-emotions-2795178

Cherry, K. (2023d, December 20). *Why communication in relationships is so important.* Verywell Mind. https://www.verywellmind.com/communication-in-relationships-why-it-matters-and-how-to-improve-5218269

Cherry, K. (2024a, May 9). *How to boost your self-awareness.* Verywell Mind. https://www.verywellmind.com/what-is-self-awareness-2795023#toc-levels-of-self-awareness

Cherry, K. (2024b, July 3). *What is empathy?* Verywell Mind. https://www.verywellmind.com/what-is-empathy-2795562

Covey, S. R. (2004). *The 7 habits of highly effective people: Powerful lessons in personal change.* Free Press.

Cuncic, A. (2024, February 12). *7 active listening techniques for better communication.* Verywell Mind. https://www.verywellmind.com/what-is-active-listening-3024343#toc-active-listening-example

Davin, K. (2022, September 12). *Impacts of lack of communication in a relationship & 13 ways to improve.* Choosing Therapy. https://www.choosingtherapy.com/lack-of-communication-in-a-relationship/

Decety, J., Bartal, I. B., Uzefovsky, F., & Knafo-Noam, A. (2016). Empathy as a driver of prosocial behaviour: Highly conserved neurobehavioural mechanisms across species. *Philosophical*

*Transactions of the Royal Society B, 371*(1686). https://doi.org/10.1098/rstb.2015.0077

Ekman, P. (1999). *Handbook of Cognition and Emotion*. Wiley.

Emmons, R. A., & Stern, R. (2013). Gratitude as a psychotherapeutic intervention. *Journal of Clinical Psychology, 69*(8), 846–55. https://doi.org/10.1002/jclp.22020

Evolve Therapy. (2023, September 11). *How your attachment style affects your communication.* Evolve Therapy MN. https://www.evolvetherapymn.com/post/how-your-attachment-style-affects-your-communication#

Eysenck, H. J. (1988), Personality, stress and cancer: Prediction and prophylaxis. *British Journal of Medical Psychology, 61*, 57–75. http://doi.org/10.1111/j.2044-8341.1988.tb02765.x

Fann, K. (2024, January 10). *5 ways to facilitate better conversations in long-term relationships.* Love What Matters. https://www.lovewhatmatters.com/better-conversations-long-term-relationships/

Favez, N., & Tissot, H. (2019). Fearful-Avoidant attachment: A specific impact on sexuality? *Journal of Sex & Marital Therapy, 45*(6), 510–523. https://doi.org/10.1080/0092623X.2019.1566946

Foulkes, L. (2021, April 28). *How to have more meaningful conversations.* Psyche. https://psyche.co/guides/how-to-have-more-meaningful-conversations

*4 communication styles & tips for communicating with each style.* (n.d.). Range. https://www.range.co/blog/communication-styles

Gill, J. (2024, February 29). *Conscious communication skills with James 'Fish' Gill | Strategies for transforming relationship conflicts* [Audio]. Spotify. https://open.spotify.com/episode/6556JNF2QKLsIMfGdmv Aeg?go=1&sp_cid=606f9dcaec09994cbb699d4ba67ffe14&utm

_source=embed_player_p&utm_medium=desktop&nd=1&dlsi=721f3d21121a40b4

Gillette, H. (2022, July 7). *Understanding what your emotions are trying to tell you.* Psych Central. https://psychcentral.com/health/understanding-what-your-emotions-are-trying-to-tell-you#emotions-scientifically-speaking

Gillis, K. (2023, June 9). *Passive–Aggressive communication: Definition, examples, and tips.* Choosing Therapy. https://www.choosingtherapy.com/passive-aggressive-communication/

Goldman, R. (2023, September 20). *What is my attachment style?* Verywell Mind. https://www.verywellmind.com/attachment-style-quiz-7562460

Gordon, A. (2016, September 15). *7 ways to make conflict healthy.* Psychology Today. https://www.psychologytoday.com/intl/blog/between-you-and-me/201609/7-ways-make-conflict-healthy

Gordon, S. (2024a, February 5). *What are the five love languages?* Verywell Mind. https://www.verywellmind.com/can-the-five-love-languages-help-your-relationship-4783538

Gordon, S. (2024b, April 14). *What does it mean to have disorganized attachment?* Health. https://www.health.com/disorganized-attachment-style-8621275#citation-13

Gottman, J. & Silver, N. (1999). *The Seven Principles for Making Marriage Work.* Crown Publishers.

Gottman, J. M., & Gottman, J. S. (2015). *Gottman couple therapy.* The Guilford Press.

Gupta, S. (2023a, February 1). *How to stop being passive-aggressive*. Verywell Mind. https://www.verywellmind.com/how-to-stop-being-passive-aggressive-7101014

Gupta, S. (2023b, September 6). *Why trust matters in your relationship and how to build it*. Verywell Mind. https://www.verywellmind.com/how-to-build-trust-in-a-relationship-5207611

Gupta, S. (2024, April 24). *How to keep a conversation going: Strategies that actually work*. Verywell Mind. https://www.verywellmind.com/how-to-keep-a-conversation-going-8637987

Hall, E. D. (2017, March 23). *Why conflict is healthy for relationships*. Psychology Today. https://www.psychologytoday.com/intl/blog/conscious-communication/201703/why-conflict-is-healthy-relationships

Harandi, T. F., Taghinasab, M. M., & Nayeri, T. D. (2017). The correlation of social support with mental health: A meta-analysis. *Electronic Physician, 9*(9).

Hollister, K. (2023, May 23). *15 powerful communication exercises for couples*. Marriage. https://www.marriage.com/advice/communication/couples-communication-boosters-top-5-activities-you-must-try/

Houston, E. (2019, April 9). *How to express gratitude to others: 19 examples & ideas*. Positive Psychology. https://positivepsychology.com/how-to-express-gratitude/

*How to read body language for better emotional awareness*. (n.d.). Calm. https://www.calm.com/blog/how-to-read-body-language

Huberman, A. (2022, October 31). *How meditation works & science-based effective meditations | Huberman Lab Podcast #96*. [Video].

YouTube. https://www.youtube.com/watch?v=wTBSGgbIvsY

Hull, R. (2016). The art of nonverbal communication in practice. *The Hearing Journal, 69*(5), 22–24. http://doi.org/10.1097/01.HJ.0000483270.59643.cc

Hundley, M. (2022, October 27). *The power of communication in a relationship.* Healing Collective Therapy. https://healingcollectivetherapy.com/resources/power-of-communication-in-a-relationship

*"I" statements communication skill.* (n.d.). Therapist Aid. https://www.therapistaid.com/therapy-worksheet/i-statements

Kardan-Souraki, M., Hamzehgardeshi, Z., Asadpour, I., Mohammadpour, R., & Khani, S. (2016). A review of marital intimacy-enhancing interventions among married individuals. *Global Journal of Health Science, 8*(8). http://doi.org/10.5539/gjhs.v8n8p74

Keohan, E. (2021, November 24). *17 communication exercises for couples' therapy.* Talk Space. https://www.talkspace.com/blog/communication-exercises-for-couples-therapy/

Kimmes, J. G., & Durtschi, J. A. (2016). Forgiveness in romantic relationships: The roles of attachment, empathy, and attributions. *Journal of Marital and Family Therapy, 42*(4), 645–658. https://doi.org/10.1111/jmft.12171

Kircanski, K., Lieberman, M. D., & Craske, M. G. (2012). Feelings into words: Contributions of language to exposure therapy. *Psychological Science, 23*(10). https://doi.org/10.1177/0956797612443830

Klynn, B. (2021, June 22). Emotional regulation: Skills, exercises, and strategies. BetterUp. https://www.betterup.com/blog/emotional-regulation-skills

Kreibig, S. D., & Gross, J. J. (2017). Understanding mixed emotions: Paradigms and measures. *Current Opinion in Behavioral Sciences, 15*, 62-71. https://doi.org/10.1016/j.cobeha.2017.05.016

Lam, C.B., Solmeyer, A.R. & McHale, S.M. (2012). Sibling relationships and empathy across the transition to adolescence. *Journal of Youth Adolescence, 41*, 1657–1670. https://doi.org/10.1007/s10964-012-9781-8

Leong, J. L. T., Chen, S. X., Fung, H. H. L., Bond, M. H., Siu, N. Y. F., & Zhu, J. Y. (2020). Is gratitude always beneficial to interpersonal relationships? The interplay of grateful disposition, grateful mood, and grateful expression among married couples. *Personality and Social Psychology Bulletin, 46*(1), 64–78. https://doi.org/10.1177/0146167219842866

Lyons-Ruth, K. (1996). Attachment relationships among children with aggressive behavior problems: The role of disorganized early attachment patterns. *Journal of Consulting and Clinical Psychology, 64*(1), 64–73. https://doi.org/10.1037/0022-006X.64.1.64

Marie, S. (2022, October 27). *How to respect other people's boundaries.* Psych Central. https://psychcentral.com/relationships/how-to-respect-other-peoples-boundaries

McKenna, K. M. (2024, January 31). How intimacy and communication are linked. Thriving Connections. https://thrivingconnectionsco.com/2024/01/how-intimacy-and-communication-are-linked/

Menanno, J. (2024). *Secure love: Create a relationship that lasts a lifetime.* Simon & Schuster.

Milek, A., Butler, E. A., Tackman, A. M., Kaplan, D. M., Raison, C. L., Sbarra, D. A., Vazire, S., & Mehl, M. R. (2018). "Eavesdropping on happiness" revisited: A pooled, multisample replication of the association between life satisfaction and observed daily conversation quantity and quality. *Psychological Science, 29*(9), 1451-1462. https://doi.org/10.1177/0956797618774252

Moghadam, M., Rezaei, F., Ghaderi, E., & Rostamian, N. (2016). Relationship between attachment styles and happiness in medical students. *Journal of Family Medicine and Primary Care, 5*(3), 593–599. http://doi.org/10.4103/2249-4863.197314

Nelson, K., & Ingalls, N. (2023, October 17). *What's your communication style? Take the quiz and find out.* Verywell Mind. https://www.verywellmind.com/take-the-communication-style-quiz-7973143

Pattemore, C. (2023, August 4). *How to set boundaries in your relationships.* Psych Central. https://psychcentral.com/relationships/why-healthy-relationships-always-have-boundaries#ineffective-boundaries

Porter, S. (n.d.). *Sustaining your relationship during major life transitions.* Lindsey Hoskins. https://lindseyhoskins.com/sustaining-your-relationship-during-major-life-transitions/

Reid, S. (2024, February 5). *Setting healthy boundaries in relationships.* Help Guide. https://www.helpguide.org/articles/relationships-communication/setting-healthy-boundaries-in-relationships.htm

Resnick, A. (2022, November 1). *It's time to ditch toxic positivity in favor of emotional validation.* Verywell Mind. https://www.verywellmind.com/it-s-time-to-ditch-toxic-positivity-in-favor-of-emotional-validation-6502330

Rowland, L., & Curry, O. S. (2019). A range of kindness activities boost happiness. *Journal of Social Psychology, 159*(3), 340–343. https://doi.org/10.1080/00224545.2018.1469461

Schaafsma, S. M., Pfaff, D. W., Spunt, R. P., & Adolphs, R. (2015). Deconstructing and reconstructing the theory of mind. *Trends in Cognitive Sciences, 19*(2), 65–72. https://doi.org/10.1016/j.tics.2014.11.007

Scheel, J. (2020, June 29). *Unconscious communication in the early stage of relationships*. Psychology Today. https://www.psychologytoday.com/intl/blog/sex-is-language/202006/unconscious-communication-in-the-early-stage-relationships

Schultz, J. (2012, December 31). *Eye contact: Don't make these mistakes*. Michigan State University Extension. https://www.canr.msu.edu/news/eye_contact_dont_make_these_mistakes

Schwartz, J. (n.d.). *How couples can turn conflict into connection*. Bayview Therapy. https://www.bayviewtherapy.com/single-post/how-couples-can-turn-conflict-into-connection

Schwartz, T. (2015, April 3). *The importance of naming your emotions*. NY Times. https://www.nytimes.com/2015/04/04/business/dealbook/the-importance-of-naming-your-emotions.html

Scott, E. (2023, December 4). *Aggressive communication: Examples and how to handle it*. Verywell Mind. https://www.verywellmind.com/what-is-aggressiveness-aggressiveness-in-communication-3145097

Selcuk, E., Stanton, S. C. E., Slatcher, R. B., & Ong, A. D. (2017). Perceived partner responsiveness predicts better sleep quality through lower anxiety. *Social Psychological and Personality Science, 8*(1), 83-92. https://doi.org/10.1177/1948550616662128

Siegel, D. (2014, December 8). *Dan Siegel: Name it to tame it.* [Video]. YouTube. https://www.youtube.com/watch?v=ZcDLzppD4Jc

Šimić, G., Tkalčić, M., Vukić, V., Mulc, D., Španić, E., Šagud, M., Olucha-Bordonau, F. E., Vukšić, M. R., & Hof, P. (2021). Understanding emotions: Origins and roles of the amygdala. *Biomolecules, 11*, 823. https://doi.org/10.3390/biom11060823

Sinclair, A. (n.d.). *How your childhood sabotaged your communication style.* Allegra Sinclair. https://allegrasinclair.com/how-childhood-sabotaged-communication-style/

Sutton, J. (2021, November 9). *Conflict resolution in relationships & couples: 5 strategies.* Positive Psychology. https://positivepsychology.com/conflict-resolution-relationships/#strategies

Tartakovsky, M. (2022, August 3). *How to be a better listener in your relationship.* Psych Central. https://psychcentral.com/relationships/listen-better-in-relationships#how-to-be-a-better-speaker

Tyng Chai M., Amin, H. U., Saad, M. N. M., & Malik, A. S. (2017). The influences of emotion on learning and memory. *Frontiers in Psychology, 8.* https://doi.org/10.3389/fpsyg.2017.01454

Wood, A. M., Froh, J. J., & Geraghty, A. W. (2010). Gratitude and well-being: A review and theoretical integration. *Clinical Psychology Review, 30*(7), 890–905. https://doi.org/10.1016/j.cpr.2010.03.005

Printed in Great Britain
by Amazon